TWENTIETH

CENTURY

BOYS

TWENTIETH CENTURY BOYS

HOW ONE FAMILY BUSINESS
SURVIVED AND THRIVED

ANDREA CLARK WATSON

SHE WRITES PRESS

Published 2021
Printed in the United States of America
Print ISBN: 978-1-64742-317-9
E-ISBN: 978-1-64742-208-0
Library of Congress Control Number: 2021911123

For information, address:
She Writes Press
1569 Solano Ave #546
Berkeley, CA 94707

She Writes Press is a division of SparkPoint Studio, LLC.

Book design by Stacey Aaronson

All company and/or product names may be trade names, logos, trademarks, and/or registered trademarks and are the property of their respective owners.

Names and identifying characteristics have been changed to protect the privacy of certain individuals.

For Mom and Dad—my role models—who together created a home filled with faith, grace, and love.

I never knew two of the four main characters in this book. My great-grandfather Si passed away long before I was born, when my dad was only two years old. My grandfather Gordon also passed away before I was born, when my oldest sister, Leslie, was two years old. Between my great-grandfather Si's tiny one-by-three-inch travel journal, my grandfather Gordon's photographs and letters, the memory of my father, Don, and the more recent history as told by my brother, Steve, I have pieced together our family history from Canada to the United States, from rural to city living, from farming to small-business ownership, through four generations.

This is a work of nonfiction. I researched time periods; read books to find details; took a trip to Leduc, Alberta; and investigated land and business documents. As an author attempting to tell a true story, I struggled with representing individuals' feelings, thoughts, and conversations when I didn't know for sure if I could correctly interpret the situations. Of course, no one alive today was there in the early 1900s to account for the conversations that happened and the thoughts and feelings associated with the actual events. But the more I learned about my great-grandparents, the more confident I felt that the words I put into their mouths were chosen with the greatest amount of accuracy and truth possible given the gap in time.

None of us have a choice of where we are born. Of course, I

am a product of my parents. I possess physical and emotional characteristics of both. But the longitude and latitude of where I took my first steps were not my choice; rather, they were the result of decisions made by my parents, my grandparents, and their parents. The house I grew up in and the community in which I was raised all had a positive and lasting impact on me, so much so that I am now raising my own kids in the same community. But what if my grandparents had never sold the farm in Canada? Or if the family business failed during the Great Depression, World War II, or the oil crisis of the 1970s? How different would my life be?

A recurring theme through each generation depicted in this book was the ambition of its members to do their own thing, separate and different from what their parents did or expected of them. I think we all have an innate desire to find our own piece of land—both literally and figuratively. But the paths we pursue and the places where we land and call home shape and provide structure not only for our own lives but for the generations that follow as well. The roads these twentieth-century boys chose—their searches, their successes and their failures—have all become part of my story.

CHAPTER ONE

1900–1902

Some journeys take us far from home.
Some adventures lead us to our destiny.
—C. S. LEWIS

THE DOOR AT THE END OF THE RAILCAR OPENED ABRUPTLY, and Si caught a whiff of lavender—a scent from home—that snapped him out of his spiraling thoughts. Within a week, he would likely be going to the church he'd grown up attending with his parents. For the first time since he'd boarded that train in Portage La Prairie, Manitoba, Si's spirits lifted ever so slightly.

Two years earlier, Si had ridden the same rails in the opposite direction with the ambition of an entrepreneur and the confidence of a lion. He had left the family farm in Watford, Ontario, to follow his dream of starting a restaurant. Eli Silas Clark (Si, as he was called) had been raised on a farm with eight siblings. Their father, Thomas, who had immigrated to Canada from Yorkshire, England, on his own as a young man, had raised the Clark children on the ideal of autonomy. Si and his siblings were encouraged to seek their own destiny, to follow their own star, and to put down roots in a place of their choosing.

From an early age, Si had a passion for food. He loved mingling spices and pairing flavors cultivated from his garden. He regularly cut recipes out of newspapers, altered them to suit his palate, and jotted down ingredients he identified when trying new foods. He had chosen Portage La Prairie, Manitoba—1,200 miles away from his hometown—as the place to open his restaurant. It was a small town, west of the capital city of Winnipeg, and a Canadian Pacific Railway stop off the Trans-Canadian Highway. It had a local newspaper and a community fair, and its population was multiplying, which made it seem like a good place to start a restaurant. Two of his sisters had settled down with families there as well.

But not long after opening, the restaurant failed. Si knew food, but he wasn't educated as a bookkeeper or manager. So, at thirty-seven years old, Si was headed back to his hometown with little to show for it except a failed attempt at his dream and a few notes scribbled into his pocket journal. When he arrived, he would be the only one of his siblings on the family farm. All eight of the others had spread out and gone on to follow their own callings.

But on this humbling trip home, Si was not in a hurry. He also loved to travel and wanted to experience the Great Lakes —Lake Superior, the Soo Locks, then Lake Huron—by steamship, instead of bypassing them by train. He hoped that the change of scenery on the six-day journey would lift his spirits and help him think about his next move, after a brief visit at home. Time was not on his side as a man of his age, and the one place he'd never imagined himself settling was the farm where he'd been raised.

On July 6, 1900, the wind blew hard. The iron-hulled steamship *Algeria* rolled from side to side as it plowed through the turbulent water of Lake Superior, creating a constant mist and causing an occasional sheet of water to curl over the bow. "The scenery is spectacular," Si wrote in the tiny journal he kept in his pocket. He traveled alone most of the time. If he didn't have a seatmate or other companion to chat with, he jotted down names of places, dates, and scenic details. In his journal he also kept the full names and birthdates of his parents, grandparents, and all his siblings. Family was important to Si.

"Two-thirds of the passengers are seasick," he wrote. Si managed to maintain his composure while a stream of pale passengers rushed by him, holding their abdomens and tossing their most recent meal into the unforgiving lake. While others fought the motion of the boat, Si kept a steady eye ahead to whatever piece of land he could spot. But he didn't focus on the horizon because he knew it would help his equilibrium, although as it turned out, it did. He focused on the landscape because he was deep in his thoughts.

Si thought about his life—where he had been, what kind of a man he was, and where he hoped he would go. He knew he didn't have all the answers. After all, he had just failed to do what he thought he was meant to do. But he also knew he wasn't done searching for his purpose, his calling, his place in the world. Having been raised in the Presbyterian Church, Si prayed silently. At that moment he wasn't fearful of the storm gaining power, or the seasickness it might bring on, or even the fierce waters of Lake Superior, which had claimed the lives of many in years past. Instead, amidst the chaos, he had a strange sense of peace and gratitude. His feelings of hope were starting to squeeze out his feelings of despair.

Once he arrived in Watford, Si relished the familiarity of home. The fields of golden wheat, almost ready to harvest, were at the peak of beauty. He'd seen them hundreds of times, but this time, they seemed even more captivating. The white two-story farmhouse that his father kept so well maintained, the porch swing, and the cluster of trees in the yard were as familiar to him as his own footprint. Home was a good place to be. But as good as it felt, Si also felt the tug of forward movement. He didn't want to let his restaurant failure define him. He still wanted to find something, somewhere to call his own.

One morning, a newspaper caught his attention: GOLD IN NOME, ALASKA, its headline read in bold black letters. It struck him instantly. He loved an adventure and could immediately visualize himself panning for gold right there on the beach in Alaska. But it wasn't just the promise of gold; the United States President William McKinley had just extended the American homesteading laws to include the Alaska Territory. On top of that, Canadian homesteads were being made available in Ontario. That was the Canadian government's plan for encouraging people to move out West. They were giving land away—free—in the areas they wanted to build up. Opportunities seemed to be beckoning him out west, and Si didn't like letting a good opportunity pass him by.

Until then, Si determined, he would appreciate the time he had with his family. Knowing Si was in town, the Fairs, longtime neighbors and family friends, invited the Clarks over for a visit. Si knew the Fair family well, but it had been many years since he had visited their house. The weeping willow out front, in all its familiarity, stood quiet. The barely detectable summer breeze was not even able to ruffle its leaves. The Fairs' two-story farmhouse with a wraparound covered porch looked exactly as he remembered. Si noted that the serenity and stillness of his hometown were so different from the clink and clang of restaurant work.

Sitting in the comfort of the shade on the porch with his parents and Mr. and Mrs. Fair, Si had a strange sensation of feeling caught between childhood and adulthood. He was in fact a grown man, but the scent of lavender and the low drone of bees buzzing around the stalks lining the white-spindled porch brought him back to his younger years and running with his friends. There was comfort in both the memories and the present.

The high-pitched squeak of the screen door as it opened turned Si's head, and for a few moments he wondered who *was* this stranger carrying the tray of biscuits. Moments later, he realized it was Annie Fair.

He could hardly believe this was the same Annie—the

youngest sister of one of his childhood friends. He remembered her as a playful child. Now, at seventeen, her rounded cheeks had thinned out, and her long braids were tied sophisticatedly on top of her head. She had an unfamiliar seriousness about her—a bit awkward, and perhaps shy. She was grown up, and Si was intrigued by her transformation.

After superficial conversation about the weather and the latest crops, the topic changed to what everyone was talking about: Nome, and the gold rush. Si told of his plans and explained that he would wait until June to start his journey to Nome since during the winter, the water would be frozen over and steamships couldn't get close enough to land. An awkward silence followed and hovered over the porch. He saw the worry in his mother's eyes and the hesitation in his father's. Annie's eyes fell to the ground and stayed there.

On July 1, 1901, Si stood on the deck of the SS *Oregon* along with 1,500 other passengers hoping to get rich on Nome's gold beaches. The mood on board was jovial and contagious. Strangers stood shoulder to shoulder, patted each other on the back, smiled and laughed together, all with the same exhilarated anticipation of going for the gold. Friends, family members, photographers, and anyone else wanting to bid them farewell stood on shore, shouting and waving as the ship pushed away.

While a few people struck it big in Nome, most came home with just enough gold to pay for the treacherous journey and have a little left over besides. While Si was one of the latter, he brought back more than just the precious metal. He brought back an experience. On his Alaskan adventure, Si had learned that the ones who profit the most are the ones who first find the treasure or are on the early end of the discovery. It's the explorers, the creators, the entrepreneurs who win. Although he didn't quite know what to do with that revelation, he knew it was important, so he held on to it.

On his return trip back to Seattle, Si felt more than ready to get back to Watford. Annie had been on his mind. She would be nineteen by the time he returned. Settling down in Watford suddenly seemed like a better option than it had a year earlier. At thirty-nine, Si's appetite for adventure was waning. He now hungered for what he had been pushing away for so many years—simplicity, security, and a home filled with family.

Back on the train, Si crossed the invisible border from the United States into Canada, marked by a wooden arch. He then traveled northeast over the Canadian Rocky Mountains. Tall and jagged, the Rockies were magnificent. But it was on the plains of Alberta that Si found the most beauty.

The Albertan plains were mostly unused land—not much to look at—but Si used his imagination. He painted golden wheat fields bordered by lines of equally spaced trees, blue skies, and glowing white farmhouses. In this picture, he even saw children playing and a wife for himself. He could likely have that in Watford, he thought. His parents were tiring of farm work and would welcome him home. Si knew he wanted that lifestyle now. But did he want it in Watford? On his parents' farm?

Halfway home, the train slowed, then stopped at the railway station in Leduc, a small town in Alberta surrounded by prairies, between the bigger cities of Calgary and Edmonton. Si looked out the window and sat a little straighter as he caught his first glimpse of this small town bursting with pride. A water tank and windmill stood on one side of the tracks, while a town center flanked a main street on the other. Leduc reminded him of his fondness for Portage La Prairie, as it, too, was on the rail line and brimming with energy.

A flyer nailed to the wall at the station read, LAST BEST WEST. Si's eyes widened as the wheels in his head started spinning. This was the Canadian government's campaign for attracting people to the rich land made available for farming in Alberta. Homesteaders seeking fulfillment of their dreams were flocking to western Canada in pursuit of their piece of free land under the Dominion Lands Act.

Suddenly, Si wanted a piece of that land. Could this be it? he wondered—free land in a small town in the plains of Alberta. There was opportunity here. He had to find out more. He felt so compelled that, as he heard the hiss of the train getting ready to depart, he jumped up and dashed off the train in Leduc, Alberta, some two thousand miles from his parents' home in Watford.

Outside the station, teams of horses pulled wagons full of

wheat down the main street of town. Farmers lined up as the waiting train blocked their path to the grain elevator on the other side of the tracks. Both single- and double-story wood-frame buildings stood side by side down the main street block. Wooden sidewalks girdled the dirt road. The Pioneer Store, Leduc Hardware, Johnson's Meat Market, Glanville General Store, and the Waldorf Hotel—the energy and urgency in that main street of Leduc was contagious. People were busy getting things done. It looked like this town was growing—a good place to be.

For a $10 administration fee, Si received a 160-acre piece of land that sat about twenty-five kilometers southwest of the town center of Leduc. Then, per the Dominion Land Act Agreement, he had three years to build a suitable dwelling and make the land farm-ready, in order to receive the title to the property.

Just a few days later, Si stood at the corner of his square plot of land southwest of Leduc. He knelt down and touched the soil. Sand, silt, and clay—ideal for growing wheat. But his plot also grew dozens of trees. After walking and surveying the whole property, Si thought about where the house would sit, and the barn, and the field. Finally, Si felt he had arrived. Here was his land—a blank slate for him to build on and make his own. He'd explored, and now he would create.

The first thing he needed to do was to erect a livable structure. Most initial structures were constructed of rough, hand-cut logs and a sod roof. The homesteaders didn't have much money at first to buy finely milled lumber for a more comfortable wood-framed house with windows. Part of the homesteading requirement was that the land had to be occupied for at least six months of the year. So until the dwelling was built, homesteaders either slept in tents on their land, or in a rooming house nearby if they could afford it.

Si looked around at the nearby plots of land. The energy he'd felt in town carried over here. Neighboring farmers got to know each other by pitching in to help in work parties called "building bees." Homesteaders took advantage of every hour of daylight to get their homes up and ready before the dark and freezing temperatures of winter brought outside work to a halt. The soil would harden under a blanket of ice and snow from November through March. Having arrived in early September, Si wouldn't be able to get a livable structure up until spring. But he had time. Getting back to Watford for the winter was what he had planned before this diversion anyway.

At the train station in Leduc, Si recalled that just a few weeks ago, when he'd jumped off the train there, he only had hope. Now he stood waiting to get back on the train with hope and land. He looked around at his fellow passengers waiting to board. There were men in three-piece suits and top hats, and others in working clothes—dark pants, long-sleeved button-up shirts, suspenders, and well-worn boots. But what drew Si's attention was a family that traveled together. The mother held the hands of a boy and a girl, one on each side, while the father spoke to the porter who stood next to a stack of trunks, presumably theirs. Si wondered if one day he would be traveling with a family—his family.

Si had always been independent, but more and more lately, strangers who became travel companions were not able to fill the void of his loneliness. Thoughts of Annie made his heart beat faster. He no longer wanted to be a single traveler. He wanted someone to enjoy life with, to stay in one place with. He hadn't left Watford with any promise to Annie, but he hoped she was still available. This journey had changed him. He was ready for the next phase of his life.

CHAPTER TWO

1902–1929

---

*There is no value in life except what you choose to place upon it,
and no happiness in any place except what you bring to it yourself.*
—HENRY DAVID THOREAU

WHILE MANY THINGS OVER THE YEARS HADN'T GONE HIS WAY,
finally Si felt his life was coming together. As he had hoped,
Annie was still single, and a few months after arriving back in
Watford, they married. At the end of the winter, the newly
married couple planned to move to Leduc, build their home,
and start their life together there.

But soon following the wedding came hints of the reality
that waited for them in Alberta. Stories of the pioneer life had
reached Annie. The hardships included families living in tiny
log cabins with leaking roofs and dirt floors, and women having to endure long, laborious work in the fields alongside the
men. Although Annie liked a bit of adventure, the prospect of
leaving her family and the comforts of the life she had known
for the conditions she had heard about frightened her.

Si also didn't really know yet what he was in for. At this

point, he didn't even have a shelter on his land. Taking risks like this hadn't fazed him as a single man. But now he had Annie to think about. He wanted the life he'd envisioned for them, but he didn't necessarily want to drag her through the mud to get there. Finally, it was decided that come spring, Si would go back to Leduc to get started on proving up his land while Annie stayed with her parents.

This time, when the train pulled into the Leduc Railway station, Si felt a combination of urgency and tranquility instead of curiosity and wonder. He had a lot to sort out, a lot to learn, and a lot of work ahead of him. But seeing the main street and the grain elevator, he felt a sense of pride in this place. His heart felt at ease and filled with affirmation that this would be the best place to start his family. He was getting closer to his dream. He had a piece of land and a possibility. He only hoped the reward would be worth the effort.

Si's property had about equal parts timber and open space. Typically, the process of homesteading followed a specific order of events. First, he needed a livable structure—just good enough to sleep in, to protect against the elements, and to procure the certificate of ownership. With the help of neighboring farmers and a few hired hands, Si had his livable structure up within a month.

The typical next step would be to clear the rest of the land for farming. Depending on the amount of timber on the land, this could take several years. The timber could be sold to the lumberyards, where it would be milled and readied for use in building a second, more refined farmhouse on the property. This was the goal for most homesteaders with families—and Si was no different. He wanted a nice house for Annie to come home to. But once Si got started selling timber, he realized there was yet another opportunity here.

Si had learned the value of timber, and the lot adjacent to his was densely forested and still available. One of the stipulations for homesteading was that if you followed the regulations and lived on your property for the required six months per year, you could also apply for another 160-acre section. By the end of his first six months, just before it was time to travel back to Annie in Watford, Si received the rights to the adjacent section of property.

Back in Watford, Si's plan to move Annie to their new homestead the following spring was thwarted by the impending birth of their first child, Gordon Fair Clark, who was born in June, 1903. That year, Annie stayed in Watford again while Si spent another six months working in Leduc.

Life for Si and Annie went on like this for the next three years, with Si spending half the year in Leduc while Annie stayed with her parents. During those years, Si never lost sight of his goal—bringing his family to the homestead. Leduc was still growing and developing into a nice community to raise a family. There, Si poured his heart into his work—selling timber, leasing parts of his land, and improving his homestead by building a more refined farmhouse—not just one good enough for shelter, but one good enough for his wife and child.

Finally, by the fall of 1905, Si had a farmhouse, a barn, and farmable land. In January of 1906, Annie gave birth to another boy, Russell Lawrence, and a few months later, the young family took up residence on their homestead in Leduc. Gordon and Russ would soon attend school in Leduc, and six years later, Si and Annie would welcome a third son, Harold Raymond, whom they would call Ray.

Si couldn't imagine a better mother of boys than Annie. She had become queen of her domain inside the house. She was not rattled by the rough-and-tumble nature of boys, but in any given minute, if the boys became quarrelsome, her calm yet firm voice could shape them up within seconds.

Life in Leduc was turning out to be not only pleasant, but prosperous. Between 1914 and 1918, wheat prices nearly doubled. Leduc was thriving, and celebrations were in abundance. In fact, the celebrating might have been too much. Excessive drinking had become such a problem in rural Alberta that Leduc joined the temperance movement, outlawing alcohol.

But despite the prohibition, the community still had a jovial spirit. Settlers threw community picnics complete with activities for the kids, such as horse races, and a pole merry-go-round at the nearby Conjuring Creek. A Leduc annual sports day included baseball, football, and hockey games for all ages.

The Clark boys were growing up happy and healthy on the

farm. Gordon, at sixteen, resembled his father, with a long forehead and ears that stuck out slightly. He had an easygoing personality and liked getting to know people. He had a knack for maintaining the agricultural equipment and enjoyed engineering contraptions that made work on the farm more efficient. He was a peacekeeper and a caretaker.

Russ, at thirteen, had a rounder face and resembled his mother. He had a seriousness about him and was the most independent-minded of the brothers. A classic middle child, Russ tended to do things his own way, and he often reminded Si of his brother Ira, who had left the family farm at seventeen and never came back. Russ was more of a thinker than a doer. He preferred using his mind to solve problems, instead of his hands on the farm. He didn't like to be told what to do, but preferred figuring things out on his own.

Ray, at eight, was the true baby of the family. He bore a strong resemblance to Gordon. But unlike his oldest brother, Ray was more trouble than help on the farm as a young boy. He was possibly the brightest of the three, but with his playful personality, he frequently found mischief. "Where is Ray?" was a common phrase around the Clark farm. Ray would often be found on a neighboring farm running around with boys his age.

Inevitably, bad times come along with good. One afternoon during the winter of 1918, Si came home from town with a copy of the *Leduc Representative*. He dropped it on the table, folded to show the page on top that read, "Deaths of the Week." Two of the fifteen names listed were neighboring farmers—a mother and child.

The Spanish flu had hit the community hard. It was awful to hear of the epidemic taking any lives in their community, but a mother and child in the same family, just a few farms away, made it all too real. Si couldn't imagine what he'd do without Annie. She had become the glue to their household.

The provincial board of health posted fliers all over town encouraging people to stay away from public meetings and crowds and including instructions on how to make a mask. Annie tended to stay close to home most of the time anyway. So when Dr. Woods, the town doctor, mentioned it might be a good idea to keep the boys home from school, Annie didn't hesitate to comply. As independent a thinker as she was, she was also a rule-follower. Fortunately, either by the grace of God or because of Annie's diligent corralling—or both—the Clark family made it through the epidemic without contracting the virus.

But their troubles weren't over yet. The heyday of high wheat prices had come to an end. Between 1919 and 1922, the price of wheat plummeted from $2.31 to $0.77 per bushel. The weather hadn't helped. A severe drought, which ended up lasting most of the decade, made for small crop yields.

By the mid-1920s, more than half of the farmhouses surrounded by the once-golden wheat fields had been abandoned, their families gone in search of better luck somewhere else. Those that remained survived on snared rabbits for meat, savored the few vegetables their gardens provided, and spent any extra pennies on flour for bread. Farming was hard work in general. But when the hard work brought little reward, it made life on the farm close to miserable. To make ends meet, Gordon and Russ—now twenty and seventeen, respectively— went to work at the nearby coal mines.

By then, the coal miners in Alberta had been through several strikes and had come out the other side, having arranged for better working conditions. Mining was still backbreaking, hard, and dirty work. But it paid nearly $7 per day, and between the two of them, Gordon and Russ were able to provide significant help to the family during difficult times. While other farmers were barely making it, the money they brought in not only allowed the Clark family to keep their farm, but also afforded them a few luxuries.

On one occasion, Gordon and Russ arrived with a new gramophone. It was a gift for their parents—one that brought Annie to tears. Si knew she didn't love the idea of her boys working in the mines, but they had made their own choice. Every night when they arrived home, Annie was visibly relieved. She loved having the whole family together, and now the mood was elevated even more by the magic of music.

The gramophone wasn't the only thing playing music. American radio was making its way to rural Alberta, glamorizing a more modern life in America. Neighbors gathered around one radio to listen to stories and to advertisements that highlighted products they had never heard of in Leduc. Si noticed that Russ was particularly fascinated with anything American, so it wasn't a huge surprise when Russ announced his plan to move to Seattle at age seventeen.

Si had always known Russ wasn't going to stick around the

family farm for very long. He recognized in him the wanderlust, the independent streak, and the desire to chase an opportunity he'd felt himself as a young man.

Russ's quick departure affected the whole family. Whether they were sad, nervous, or envious, the day-to-day energy on the farm felt different. Si noticed that it was Gordon who'd seemed the most hurt when Russ announced his plan. Gordon was more of a pleaser than Russ. He had always just done what needed to be done on the farm, without question or complaint. As the oldest, Si expected him to adopt more and more of the responsibility, and now that Russ was gone, Si needed Gordon more than ever.

To make matters worse, the drought continued. Over the years, Si had learned not to fret too much about things he couldn't control—mainly the weather. But the drought had become a seemingly unending threat, and he couldn't help but worry. On top of that, wheat prices hadn't yet rebounded. The first half of the 1920s had been grim both economically and emotionally, and unfortunately, 1926 did not start out any better.

One spring day, Annie couldn't get out of bed. She didn't often get sick, and rarely complained of pain, so when she couldn't stand up without doubling over, Si called for Dr. Woods. By the time he arrived, Annie was hot with fever and had a swollen belly. Dr. Woods's diagnosis was appendicitis, but since their small hospital in Leduc did not do surgeries, she had to be rushed to the closest city, Edmonton, about twenty miles away. Annie spent more than a week in Edmonton after surgery, then was then sent home to recover under the care of Dr. Woods.

Once home, Annie seemed to be recovering slowly, until one morning, she wouldn't wake up. Si called for Dr. Woods immediately. Annie still had breath, but she had slipped into a coma, likely the result of a blood clot—a complication from surgery. A day later, on July 17, 1926, Annie passed away in her home. She was forty-six years old.

Grief flattened Si. He couldn't function on the farm, or in the kitchen, or as a parent. Annie had been the family's anchor. She held everything together, and everyone in their place. She had brought life onto the farm when before it was just a piece of land. She *was* life on the farm, and now Si didn't know how he would continue without her.

On top of his grief, Si was now in his sixties. Work on the farm had stolen his energy. He was tired. Over the prior few years, he had been delegating more of the responsibility to Gordon. After Russ left, Gordon had taken over the bulk of the work anyway, but now Si didn't even feel like helping. Ray wasn't much help either. He had continued on to high school —unlike his older brothers who had stopped after eighth grade—but now, perhaps due to his mother's absence, Ray was becoming more difficult, and Si didn't know what to do with him. It felt like an impossible situation.

Then one day, Ray's school teacher visited. "Si, Ray has been drinking at school again. He is causing a lot of trouble." Si hung his head low with guilt and regret. He didn't know what else to say or do. He knew Ray missed his mother terribly. He'd been only fifteen when she died, and Si had failed to give him the same nurturing care as Annie had. In his sadness, anger, and boredom with rural life, Ray, now eighteen, had turned to drinking.

Later that evening, Gordon approached Si about the situation. "We have to do something about Ray," he said. "This isn't working anymore. I can't keep up with the work. Something needs to change."

"I know." Si felt defeated. He missed Annie during times like these.

"I think it's time to sell the farm. Ray needs a change. We all need a change." Gordon spoke with gentle authority, as if he'd been rehearsing the conversation. Si had considered selling the farm, too, but in his grief, and given his age, the thought had overwhelmed him. But this was Gordon's idea. Once Gordon spoke the words, Si let out the breath he had been holding for years. For the first time in a long time, he felt a huge sense of relief. It was time for a fresh start.

As a homesteader, Si had brought his family out West for the open space, the opportunity, and the freedom to run. The same thing that had satisfied his own wanderlust was now inhibiting or proving detrimental to his sons. They deserved to have their own dreams. They deserved to make their own way without feeling the guilt of leaving the family farm. His three sons possessed differing amounts of courage, perseverance, and loyalty, but they had the same ambitions that he recalled in himself at their age.

Si knew that through no one's fault, no one's failures, it had come to this. Life was changing, and they needed to change, too.

It was time to sell the farm.

CHAPTER THREE

1929

Making a decision was only the beginning of things. When someone makes a decision, he is really diving into a strong current that will carry him to places he had never dreamed of when he first made the decision.

—PAULO COELHO

GORDON HAD ALWAYS BEEN GOOD AT FARM WORK AND HADN'T thought about any other life for himself until after Russ announced his exit plan. He felt cheated at first, as if his younger brother had cut in front of him in line at the bank. Then the letters started coming, describing Russ's life in Seattle, with opportunities so plentiful they could be picked up at the corner newsstand.

But even if Gordon could have mustered up the courage to go, he felt stuck after his mother's death and his father's advancing age. He could certainly envision a different life for himself—maybe in business—but Gordon was loyal. He had responsibilities—family responsibilities on the farm he couldn't leave behind.

The trouble with Ray was the catalyst that allowed a daring but perfect plan to come together. It was a way to keep the family intact and put Gordon in a place where he could explore a non-farming way of life. He was twenty-six years old, and it was time for him to take charge of his life. Just like his father, Gordon wanted to find that something to call his own. He would just need to take Si and Ray with him.

The farm, the animals, and all the equipment sold for $6,900 (which equates to a little over $100,000 today). Included in the sale were the gramophone and gramophone records. The gift that once brought so much joy had been collecting dust in the years since Annie's passing. Although it had become a memento of happy times together amid the hardship of farming on the plains of Canada, separating the gramophone from the house didn't seem right. It was conveyed with the sale, but Gordon would always treasure it. While the memories of some objects disappear as soon as we no longer possess them, others we feel in our hearts far longer than we actually felt them in our hands.

With enough money to reach Seattle and the rest in the bank of Canada until it was needed, they loaded Gordon's 1926 Buick sedan, taking only the personal belongings they could fit in the car. Gordon drove, Si took the passenger seat, and Ray rode in back—symbolic of the roles they now had.

As Gordon drove away, he felt sad to leave, but ready to go. Si sat in silence, looking out the window. Gordon knew what he was thinking. His dad had traveled on that road toward Leduc thousands of times over the last twenty-nine years. He knew each landowner for as far as he could see. Each farm was separated by a dirt road and shrubbery or a line of tall trees. So much remained the same, yet so much had changed. The farm marked Si's greatest accomplishment. He had literally transformed a piece of raw land, dense with trees, into his livelihood, his family home, and a dream come true.

Gordon sensed mixed feelings from Ray, who also sat quietly in the back seat. He wasn't sure whether Ray felt sad to leave the only home he'd ever known, or if he felt elated that they were finally quitting the place that had turned so dismal since his mother died. Although Ray's behavior had been the final deciding factor, Gordon made sure Ray understood that selling the farm was the right thing to do for all of them. He wanted to free Ray of any guilt, leaving only good memories behind.

With the farm at their backs, they had one stop to make before heading south: the Leduc cemetery, where they would say a last goodbye to Annie. Si brought flowers cut from his garden—roses, her favorite flower. He had visited Annie's grave every time he had an errand in Leduc. He talked to her there. Gordon knew that leaving Leduc would be hardest on his father for this reason.

Vines etched in various shades of gray wrapped around her name, Annie Fair Clark, on the stone. "We sold the farm, Annie, we're leaving Leduc . . . for a while, anyway." Si took off his fedora, held it to his chest and knelt down in front of her concrete headstone. Gordon heard his father's hesitation about "leaving Annie" when he'd initially brought up moving to the United States, but it wasn't until this moment that Gordon felt he really understood what Si meant. He had brought his young wife, somewhat reluctantly, to Leduc, and now he was leaving without her.

Ray broke the silence. "We're going to Seattle, Ma. We'll be near Russ," he chimed in, as if trying to justify their actions. Ray might have been the most scarred by his mother's absence, but he still wanted to please her, and he knew how much she loved having the family together.

"We'll be back to visit," added Gordon as he put his hand on Ray's shoulder. He wasn't exactly sure whom he was addressing: his mother, his father, his younger brother, or himself. Maybe all four, as a way of convincing them and himself that this *was* the right thing to do. In his mother's final moments, he'd had to be strong for both his father and his younger brother. He'd wept only briefly and in private at her deathbed and fought back tears during this final goodbye at her grave.

On the road, Gordon turned his thoughts to what could be ahead. Russ had written about the indoor plumbing, the convenience of electricity, the hustle on the streets, and the restaurants. The rooming house where he lived was a fraternity of likeminded men who had also left their families in search of their own independence. There were electric streetlights dangling on a line high above the streets, unpleasant and pleasant smells, and a plethora of modern cars. It was so drastically different from the pace of life on the farm. Russ's life had moved forward quickly and for the better, so it seemed.

Within months of arriving, Russ had started taking business classes in Seattle while working his job at Texaco. In one of his classes, he met an independent-minded woman from Montana, who was living in a ladies' rooming house nearby. Beulah was not like the girls Russ had known in rural Canada, nor was she the type that displayed inappropriate behavior like so many he'd seen in the city at night. Beulah was attractive, smart, and also had a sense of adventure. She had come to Seattle for the same reasons as Russ—to get away from her hometown, her parents' rules, and to create her own destiny.

Six months after they started dating, on Christmas Day 1925, Russ and Beulah married in Montana. A couple years later, they bought a house in Rainier Valley, an area in the southeast part of Seattle, bordered by Lake Washington to the east.

In May of 1929, Gordon, Si, and Ray arrived at the United States–Canadian border in Surrey, British Columbia. Gordon watched Si's posture change as he stood in Peace Arch Park looking at the monument that straddled the invisible line between the two countries. Si had told the boys about his Gold Rush days and specifically remembered passing through the then-small wooden arch built right over the tracks, when, soon after, he had stumbled upon Leduc. Gordon worried this memory would trigger sadness in Si about leaving his country of birth, but instead it seemed to prompt hope and optimism he hadn't seen in his dad since his mother passed away.

A British Union Jack and a United States flag stood on top of the peace arch, each on its respective side. In the portal mounted on the wall was an iron gate, and above it the words

MAY THESE GATES NEVER BE CLOSED. The three of them walked around and through the peace arch, taking it all in. Gordon had both confidence and apprehension as he stood there looking at the border. He was leaving one country and entering another. He was also leaving one life and starting another.

Once in Seattle, they drove south and east of downtown, to the Rainier Valley area. The spring Seattle sky held thick layers of clouds, ranging from cotton-white to battleship-gray, with sky-blue patches in between. The uncertainty of the weather mirrored the feeling in the Buick that day. Red bricks paved each side of the train tracks and added a welcome splash of color. The space between the rails, holding puddles of muddy water, suggested a recent rain, while the clouds overhead threatened another. People in Seattle moved with purpose, their energy palpable.

A lofty wooden building sitting cockeyed on the right-hand side of Rainier Avenue caught Gordon's eye. Stewart Lumber and Hardware looked like a place a do-it-yourself guy like him would frequent. Cars of all types were parked outside the building—Chevy roadsters, Buick coupes, and Ford Model A's. The scene was intriguing, and just as Russ had described. Gordon loved cars. He took pride in his own car, making sure to keep it clean. He anticipated every new model, and relished tinkering with the latest accessories.

A streetcar approached, heading north on Rainier Avenue. It held a big sign affixed to its front end that read, BASEBALL TO-DAY. It was game day for the Seattle Indians. Although Ray kept quiet, Gordon could feel his younger brother's excitement as they moved further along. Ray's eyes fixated on the left side of the street, and his jaw dropped open when he saw what was there. With its double-decker stadium seating and enormous electric lights, Dugdale Park was the grandest ballpark any of them had ever seen. Ray was a fun-loving teenager, but in rural Canada, there had only been pick-up games. Living in Seattle would be his first opportunity to experience professional baseball.

When they reached the top of the hill, they arrived in the neighborhood known as Columbia City, one of several that made up the long, narrow Rainier Valley district. Shops lined both sides of the street. Gordon parked the car in front of the Columbia Confectionery. In the window, signs read ICE CREAM TO TAKE HOME, and TASTY CHEWING GUM FOR ONE CENT. A sweet tooth was something all the Clark men shared.

Although Columbia City had been annexed to Seattle in 1907, the area still maintained a small-town look and feel. It was a community that, like Leduc, had its own newspaper, the *Rainier Valley Times*. A large ad in the latest issue endorsed the local streetcars, saying "Welcome New Neighbors," an indication that this was a growing area.

This was the sort of place that held annual parades and festivals complete with pony rides, a merry-go-round, and musical performances, and where merchants and businessmen gathered in the banquet room at the Columbia Café to discuss local commerce. The paper even said, "Rainier District Friends: A friend in need is a friend indeed," and went on to list all the ways people in the community helped each other.

Over the years Gordon had heard stories of how his father had felt when he'd first spotted the opportunity in Leduc. He wondered if his own feelings right then were similar. In this first journey down Rainier Avenue, Gordon saw opportunity. He saw a community of people that helped each other, and he sensed positive energy within the people. Columbia City felt like what Si had described about Leduc, but it was more bustling and progressive and fresh to his senses. This was a place worth calling home, Gordon decided, and he hoped Si and Ray felt the same way.

He remembered the words spoken by recent past President Calvin Coolidge: "After all, the chief business of the American people is business. They are profoundly concerned with producing, buying, selling, investing, and prospering in the world." While Seattle seemed promising at this point, Gordon wondered if a Canadian farmer could survive in this American business world.

CHAPTER FOUR

1929

Life is complex. Each one of us must make his own path through life. There are no self-help manuals, no formulas, no easy answers. The right road for one is the wrong road for another.

—M. SCOTT PECK

A FEW DAYS LATER, IN THEIR APARTMENT ON 38TH AND Angeline Streets, Gordon's eyes popped open before dawn as usual. He was used to rising early on the farm, and this habit had been hard to shake, even on the mornings he didn't have anything to get up for. The fact that his dad and younger brother slept under the same roof seemed like the only constant from mornings back in Leduc. Street noise had replaced the rooster calls. The fields, the tractors, the barn, the animals—Gordon found himself thinking about the long list of tasks he wouldn't be doing. The hard, physical labor he had felt so ready to leave behind now struck him as less intimidating than the unfamiliarity that each day now held in store. But there was no going back. He didn't have anything to go back to. Change is hard, Gordon had realized, even when you choose it.

Russ's familiarity with people and the area helped. Within a month of their arrival, Russ had contacted friends and helped secure a job for Ray at the Port of Seattle. Getting Ray settled in a job sooner rather than later was as much about helping him acclimate to life in the city as it was keeping him busy and out of trouble. If Ray could find mischief in rural Canada, he would certainly be able to find it in the Rainier Valley. Rumor had it that the local teenagers were known to occasionally smother the streetcar tracks with grease, then watch the streetcar known as "Dinky" struggle to get up the hill or slow to make the turn at 50th and Genesee without derailing.

But Ray might have been beyond that type of mischief anyway. It seemed that getting Ray out of Canada had been exactly what he needed. Almost overnight, he had transformed from an uninterested teenager who couldn't stay out of trouble to a responsible deck hand at Fisherman's Terminal with aspirations of his own. Ray marveled every day at the number of containers full of salmon, halibut, cod, and shellfish that came off the fishing vessels. He had stories to tell and overheard conversations to repeat after his workday at home with Si and Gordon. Ray had suddenly grown up.

Settling in for Si had been just as easy. If the move added a couple years of maturity for Ray, it actually had the opposite effect on Si. Without any responsibilities, Si was a younger man with a new pair of walking shoes. He quickly settled into a bit of a weekly routine, the most important part of which was on Saturday, when the Columbia Confectionery made its famous peanut brittle. He smiled more, stood taller, and walked around town with carefree confidence. Gordon wasn't sure if he'd ever known this relaxed and contented version of his dad.

At times, Gordon felt a pang of envy. It was a reversal of fate that both Ray and Si had made such a smooth transition, while Gordon struggled. But he had to remind himself that he really didn't want it any other way. Now, instead of worrying about them, he could focus on himself.

Figuring out what to do next became a constant effort for Gordon. He felt the weight of the unknown and the pressure to settle into a routine. Gordon liked routine. It provided the structure he needed to feel like he was accomplishing something. It was OK with him if the daily routine needed to be altered. He wasn't so rigid that he couldn't be spontaneous, but he liked waking up in the morning with a clear idea of what needed to be done, and he liked checking things off his mental list. This was a drill he hadn't anticipated missing. He knew he would need to be patient in finding a job he wanted, or perhaps a business to buy, but what he hadn't expected was that the lack of daily, purposeful direction would be so uncomfortable.

As the days went on, while Si let his taste buds lead him through the Rainier Valley, Gordon became driven by a different agenda—getting to know the business owners. He noted that they took pride in their work and appreciated the local clientele. He found himself picturing life in their shoes. He loved talking to people. Like his father, Gordon could strike up a conversation with just about anyone, and often did. He quickly learned names and always used them when greeting people. While buying a newspaper at the newsstand, he would say, "Well hello there, Gus. How's business today, my friend?"

In getting to know people, Gordon started to feel more a part of the community, but still, there were days when he felt he was aimlessly wandering, getting nowhere in his search for *that* job. He was seeking a job that wasn't just any job, but a business—one that satisfied his desires. He didn't know exactly what he was looking for, or how he would find it, but he knew he wanted something to call his own—something to be proud of. He wanted to stake his claim in *the business of America*, the same way his father had once staked his claim in the new Canadian territory. But as concrete as this dream felt, as vividly as he could picture himself there, the path to making it a reality remained elusive. As time went on, his confidence waned. Thoughts of regret and leaving the only life he knew—even in its monotonous simplicity—still haunted him from time to time.

Counteracting Gordon's intermittent feeling of discouragement was the momentum of Seattle's thriving culture, which pushed him to continue. When he allowed it to, the energy of the city invigorated him. Seattle was growing in the late 1920s. In the prosperous economy, people were starting businesses, making money, and spending it freely. They came by boat, train, car, and now airplane, landing at Seattle's new passenger airport, Boeing Field. The extravagant Olympic Hotel had expanded and was having no trouble filling its elegant rooms. The University of Washington saw a dramatic increase in enrollment, which jumped from 3,000 to 8,500 in just a few years. And, inventions were being made. Don Ibsen, a Franklin High School student, nailed a pair of tennis shoes to sanded and bent cedar planks, and after a series of experiments on Lake Washington, contributed to the invention of water skis. This was where innovation happened, and it was exciting.

Gordon still felt Seattle was the right place to be, even if his adjustment was a bit slow. It seemed to be the center of all things business, although he was still an outsider. He wanted to get in, to be a part of that. He wanted to be one of those Seattle businessmen. *But how?* he wondered. *How does a Canadian farmer step into the American business world?*

If growing up as a farmer had taught Gordon anything, it was that after the hard work, it came down to patience and faith. Regardless of how well one planted the seeds and farmed the land, only God controlled the weather that ultimately determined the success of the crop. Now living in Seattle, Gordon had to redirect his patience and faith as it applied to his current situation. He had already done the hard work of pulling up the family roots and moving. He knew he wanted to be a businessman. He was in the right place. Now he just needed to be patient and trust that the right opportunity would come along—hopefully sooner rather than later.

Months passed. Gordon sat across the kitchen table from Russ and next to Beulah in their modest Rainier Valley home. Accordioned cigarette butts branded with lipstick crowded the copper ashtray on the table. The cherry lit up as Beulah inhaled from a new one, then tilted her head slightly toward the ceiling and elegantly blew out the smoke.

Smoking cigarettes—especially for women—hadn't been as common in Leduc as it was in Seattle. But Beulah was a progressive, independent, modern woman. Her drop-waist dress with a lacy collar just barely covered her knees. She wore her hair short, cut in a boyish bob with "s"-shaped waves lying flat against her head.

Russ had grown up in the same household as Gordon—a middle-class farm boy. But after marrying Beulah, it seemed as if Russ had stepped up a rung on the social ladder. She brought a more sophisticated, modern aspect to the relationship, which both puzzled and amused Gordon.

Still, Gordon was proud of what his brother had done since leaving the farm six years prior. Back then, he'd still seen Russ as his kid brother who knew a little about a lot of things, but not a lot about anything. Since Russ had lived in Seattle, he seemed to have grown up, and almost acted the role of the older brother now. He certainly had more culturally relevant experience in Seattle and knew a lot of important businessmen in the area. Gordon looked up to Russ for guidance in that respect. But when it came to family matters, Russ knew Gordon was the peacekeeper, the one who kept the family together.

"Dad and Ray still doing all right?" Russ asked that question frequently. So frequently, in fact, that it was starting to get on Gordon's nerves. *They* were doing fine. It was Gordon who was still grappling to find his purpose. But he didn't let that show. Gordon wore stress and worry neatly tucked up his sleeve.

"Yeah, we're all getting along fine," Gordon said. He preferred to put on an act of contentment even when he didn't feel it.

Relieved, Russ sat back in his chair. "You know John Scott's looking to sell his business."

"John Scott? The service station?" Gordon knew it well. A mechanic's shop with a gas pump, a two-bay garage, and a small five-by-eight-foot structure as the office. It was just a few blocks down from his apartment, on the corner of Genesee and 37th. He stopped there for gas and the occasional consultation about his car. In fact, he had started frequenting the service station every few days, not because he needed anything, but just because he liked talking to the mechanics or any other customers there filling up. It was at the service station that Gordon also learned about the popular places to go on a Sunday drive, such as Port Townsend, Bainbridge Island, or east to the mountains on Snoqualmie Pass or to Mount Rainier.

"That's the one. The coal yard next door is for sale, too. John Scott owns them both. The building across the street is his office. He's selling them together," said Russ, as he tapped his empty coffee cup on the table and looked at Beulah. She got right up and brought back the half-full coffee pot. She was sophisticated, smart, and more modern in her choice of clothing and accessories, but still traditional in the role of a wife.

Being his own boss was what Gordon had always really

wanted. It was the lofty goal he was almost afraid to say out loud, for fear it might not happen. He had been willing to put that desire aside for a time while he got his bearings in Seattle. But having his own business someday was always his aim. He had known that for years. It hadn't occurred to Gordon until that moment that he and Russ could be business partners. Suddenly, the whole idea of owning a business felt more tangible.

Russ sat up, put both forearms on the table, and leaned toward Gordon. "It's really one business, with two services. Interesting business, the two of those together. I imagine the coal business keeps him busy in the winter while the service station keeps him busy in the summer, if not all year."

Gordon's mind was racing. This was exciting. He had a knack for mechanics, so the service station was attractive. He'd fixed all his family's farm equipment, and the neighbors', too. He preferred figuring out how to maintain his own car engine over paying someone else to do it. The coal business sounded interesting, too. Winters in Seattle were cold, so heat was a basic need. Coal had become the preferred, most popular source of heat for homes in the area.

Over the next few weeks, conversations continued between Gordon and Russ. Herbert Hoover's recent campaign slogan, "A chicken in every pot, and a car in every garage," had them thinking that a service station would be a good business in this economy. More cars meant more need for services. Moreover, in any economy, people needed heat, so the coal business should be a sure thing.

They consulted John Scott and discussed the logistics of running two businesses. John confirmed that together, the two kept him busy all year long. The coal business thrived in winter, when people needed to heat their homes. Trucks loaded with coal ran up and down the neighborhood streets all season long, dropping loads down the coal chutes that most residential buildings were equipped with. The chutes led straight to the basement, where the homeowner would manually shovel coal into the furnace all winter, as needed. As soon as spring came, people in Seattle turned off their furnaces and enjoyed going on drives to nearby islands or the mountains, therefore needing gas or maintenance at the service station.

This business, like farming, was also dependent on weather. A good cold winter in the coal business—John Scott told them —could set their finances for the whole year. But a warm winter could be detrimental without smart financial planning. The number of unknowns based on the unpredictability of the weather was why John Scott was ready to sell the business. He preferred concrete, tangible stability, such as real estate.

Si became involved in the conversations along the way as well. It was, after all, the money from Si's farm that would fund the business. Although Gordon and Russ were now making most of the family decisions, including financial ones, they valued their dad's opinion. Every endeavor has risks. Regardless of how much research, due diligence, and best/worst case scenario thought processes one goes through, at some point every business venture has to take a leap of faith. Si fully knew that, based on his own failures and successes. Gordon and Russ understood the risk, too, and it was a big risk. The price of John Scott's businesses was most of their money. There would be little left if it failed.

The volatile September weather, with its mix of sun and rain, paralleled the blend of reverie and uncertainty Gordon felt. After weeks of mulling over the pros and cons, Gordon found himself walking on Genesee Street. He stopped between John Scott's service station on his right, and the office building of Genesee Coal & Stoker on his left. Now that what seemed like the perfect opportunity had come along, Gordon felt a hesitation that surprised him.

As he stood there, many thoughts swirled through his head. So many things had changed in such a short period of time. Looking forward, so much was still unknown. Despite his careful calculations, Gordon worried whether spending all his family's money on this businesses was truly wise. Part of him had doubts about working together with Russ. It wasn't the way he had imagined becoming a businessman. Some of his recent memories of working together on the farm were not so rosy, though maybe the idea of cooperating brought back the memory of happier times when their mother was with them. Regardless, despite the risks, Gordon kept moving toward the idea that this business would work.

Gordon was so deeply involved in his thoughts that he

didn't hear the streetcar, with its heavy load of coal, screeching as it rounded the corner behind him. He did not know how long he had been standing there, debating with himself about how this would work, when the coal car arrived to interrupt his gaze. Although he stood still, life marched on around him. He had to choose to put one foot in front of the other and to move in faith. Faith and family.

Business agreements back then were not done through a bank. The parties to a deal typed up sale agreements and signed them, but the transfer of money for the duration of the agreement was between businessmen. The brothers concluded that they could pay John Scott a portion of the sale price and then set up monthly payments of $150 to him for the remainder, just as they had done on the sale of the farm.

Then, on the foundation of trust, Russ and Gordon shook hands with John Scott and signed a contract. They were business partners now. It was a family business. Gordon hoped their personality differences would prove complementary, not catastrophic.

CHAPTER FIVE

1929–1931

Trouble shared is trouble halved.
—LEE IACOCCA

IN EARLY OCTOBER 1929, WHILE THE NORTHWEST FALL WEATHER turned cool, the national economy still ran hot. The stock market seemingly had no ceiling, and the Seattle drizzle hadn't yet arrived to dampen the mood. A new feeling of American pride now burst within Gordon. Surely it was that same sense of pride he had recently witnessed filling up and spilling over the other local American businessmen he had gotten to know in his first few weeks after arriving in Seattle. Suddenly Gordon felt a kinship with them, one he didn't need a birth certificate to prove.

The words of President Hoover's inaugural speech were becoming unequivocally true: "Ours is a land rich in resources; stimulating in its glorious beauty; filled with millions of happy homes; blessed with comfort and opportunity. In no nation are the institutions of progress more advanced. In no nation are the fruits of accomplishment more secure. In no nation is the government more worthy of respect. No country is more loved by its people. I have an abiding faith in their capacity, integrity, and high purpose. It is bright with hope." Gordon felt the truth of these words; he believed his future *was* bright.

That energetic, optimistic atmosphere helped fuel Russ and Gordon's confidence, and they got right to work, sparing no expense. Their first order of business was changing their signage. The Genesee Service Station sign was fine, but adding "Clark Brothers Properties" in smaller print below would establish them as an up-and-coming business presence in the neighborhood. After all, they owned other properties as well. The office of Genesee Coal & Stoker sat just across the street on the corner of 37th and Genesee.

Right away Gordon and Russ fell into responsibilities and tasks that aligned with their natural strengths. Gordon spent most of his time at the service station. He loved developing relationships with customers and talking to them about their cars. He could identify every make and model just by looking at the grill. When a new one, hot off the assembly line, pulled into his station, he'd nearly spring out of his shoes with delight to check out the modern features the latest model had to offer. Of course, he always struck up conversation with his customers.

"Good looking car. Brand-new, huh?" Gordon asked, admiring a Ford Model A convertible while he assisted the customer with checking his oil level under the hood.

"That's right. Just had her for a month," the customer replied, oozing with pride. The chrome around the headlights and the grill sparkled in the sunlight. The muted yellow paint, flawless. The red wheels were a popular choice, but not Gordon's preference. He liked white.

"Just out for a Saturday drive? Beautiful day for it," Gordon said, nodding toward the man's wife in the passenger seat, and noticing a picnic basket and folded wool blankets sitting on the rumble seat in back.

"Yes, thought we'd drive up to Paradise Inn on Mount Rainier. This might be the last chance to see the fall colors before they go," he replied.

"Sounds like a good idea. Winter is coming." Gordon knew he didn't have time for much travel yet, but he kept suggestions from conversations like this in his back pocket, for another day. Mount Rainier, Lake Chelan, and the Oregon Coast were all places he looked forward to visiting, and he hoped one day he would have a wife sitting in his own passenger seat.

Meanwhile, Russ got to work on the books, managing the employees and the coal-delivery schedules. Although Gordon was the older brother, he knew Russ liked to be in charge, so he let him. The brothers had inherited three trucks with the business. Gordon made sure the trucks were always clean and looking sharp. The exterior condition of the trucks was important to him—it was what the customers saw driving around their neighborhoods and sitting in front of their homes. A well-maintained truck indicated a well-run business. Gordon worked toward having the best-looking trucks in the neighborhood, while Russ worked on running the best fuel company in the business. It was like pen and ink. Different functions, but both necessary for the desired outcome.

Just a few months in, it became apparent that the two-business model that had initially concerned the brothers was in fact ideal. The arrangement allowed them to compartmentalize yet work together. The fact that the businesses operated separately, physically divided by Genesee Street, made it even better. Each brother had his own space—Gordon in the service station and Russ in the office of the coal business— but they were also tied together with an invisible shoestring.

During the spring and summer of 1929, the Seattle economy had been better than anyone could have imagined, and even now it was still growing. The stock market was the talk of the town. It had reached an all-time high, plateauing briefly in August before recharging and furthering its climb. People had money to spend, and they spent it without hesitation.

Life in the 1920s was full of fashion, good times, new inventions, and the idea that anyone could make money, and lots of it. By late in the decade, even simple folks had gotten in on the stock market hype. People invested on margins, or with their life savings, or took out loans to buy more shares in a stock market that just kept getting better. All Gordon and Russ's money, however, was tied up in the business—a more tangible bet, if they were to call themselves gambling men. But still, they did get in on the spending spree.

Now a true businessman, Gordon wanted to look the part. A good businessman needs a good suit, he thought. A loyal man, Gordon believed in doing business with those who did business with him—in the same way Si had traded with other farmers in Leduc even when he could have afforded to spend cash. This sense of customer loyalty quickly became a cornerstone and mantra for business with Gordon. He immediately bought a new Fahey-Brockman three-piece suit, black, with pinstripes, from a new coal customer, Philip Fahey of Fahey-Brockman Clothiers. An investment, Gordon thought, well worth the expense.

Gordon and Russ were feeling good about how their lives were unfolding. Things had fallen right into place. Ray was happy at his job and staying out of trouble. Si was happy and within arm's length of all his boys. Gordon especially felt ecstatic that this move to Seattle was working out exactly the way he had dreamed.

It almost felt too good to be true.

Then, on October 23, 1929, shocking news arrived. The newspapers announced that the New York Stock Exchange had taken a drastic dive. Over the weeks that followed, the stock market fell, and fell, and fell.

Panic waves rippled across the country.

Of course, no one had any way of knowing this event would launch them into a recession so big that it would later come to be called the Great Depression. At first, the only people directly affected by the crash were the ones with all their money in the stock market. Newspapers ran photos of well-dressed businessmen with signs on their fancy cars that read, FOR SALE, LOST EVERYTHING IN THE STOCK MARKET.

Although the news was distressing, it did not undo most

people in Seattle just yet. Gordon knew the crash was big, and that it had created a sense of panic regardless of personal investments. But for the most part, he didn't know what to think about this development. He, like most people, didn't fully understand how something so intangible would eventually affect people in Seattle. Some didn't believe it ever would, and carried on with business as usual.

A headline in the October 29 *Seattle Times* read, "STOCKS HIT LOWEST LEVELS." Just below that, the president of the Bon Marché department store was quoted: "We're planning a tremendous Christmas this year. Last year was the biggest in our history. This year we expect far to surpass it."

When Gordon picked up the newspaper that day, he gave the headlines some thought, and an audible *hmmm.* Sometimes he found interesting articles in the paper worthy of cutting out and keeping. But news of the crash didn't warrant that. What was catching his eye lately were advertisements for Gladstone Bags, with pictures of businessmen holding something that resembled a doctor's medical bag. This stiff leather satchel with a rigid hinged frame and a buckle on top was one of the accessories that helped differentiate upper-class professionals from simple working-class folks. Gordon wanted his to be adorned with his initials, G. F. C. This bag would be another worthwhile investment for a good businessman.

As the fall of the stock market continued to make news, however, Gordon and Russ started to wonder what this development would mean for them as the weather got colder. They took note of the community musings, read the papers, and contemplated the opinions being voiced by other Rainer Valley merchants. *We'll be fine*, Gordon thought. *Our business shouldn't be affected much, if any. We provide fuel, and everyone needs fuel.* Still, he couldn't help but wonder.

But winter was approaching fast, and the brothers really didn't have time to think much about the news. They'd barely been able to keep up with learning all they needed to know about their new business when the cold, dark, and shorter days of midwinter kick-started furnaces that sputtered for fuel, thrusting the Clark brothers into high gear.

December had been busy, but soon after the new year, in January 1930, Seattle was hit with one of the longest, most bone-chilling cold snaps ever recorded in the area. The cold weather went on and on. Temperatures stayed well below freezing for so long, it turned Seattle's Green Lake into a solid mass of ice, thirteen inches thick. This was so novel that one day, a bunch of daring youngsters drove a car from one end of Green Lake to the other and back, successfully confirming the breadth and depth of the ice. Then, like ants that'd had their marching orders revoked, eager witnesses flooded the ice, slipping and sliding in every direction. Soon skaters arrived, bonfires were assembled, hot chocolate stands were erected, and musicians hoping to earn a few coins set up to entertain. It was described in the newspaper as "Mardi Gras on Green Lake." The festive atmosphere went on for weeks and weeks, bringing a much-needed silver lining to the long, frigid winter.

But Gordon and Russ didn't have time for ice skating or even to glance at the snowmen in their neighbors' backyards.

This was their first winter in the heating business, and they were being put to the test. Fortunately, although the weather felt relentless, the customers were grateful for the service they had to offer. Heat was one of their most basic needs, and despite the stress of Gordon and Russ's learning curve, Genesee Coal & Stoker successfully provided.

By fall of 1930, attitudes had changed. People in Seattle were no longer wearing confidence like a tailored suit. They were clutching their wallets and just hoping to keep their jobs. Evidence of the fallen economy was everywhere. Everyone felt it. Fewer customers had visited the service station that summer, as driving for pleasure was a luxury many could no longer afford. By the beginning of December, it was already clear that fewer customers were buying coal. After last winter's epic freeze, customers nervously allowed thin layers of frost to build up on their window panes. They were still feeling the pain of having had to spend so much money for heat the winter before. They feared another hard winter and felt determined to weather the cold as long as they could, rather than spending money they could ill afford to lose.

As the months passed, the downturned economy wasn't rebounding. In fact, it was getting even worse. Although that winter didn't end up breaking records, it also didn't loosen people's purse strings. The brothers' coal business was surviving, but its future was becoming increasingly uncertain. They had started off strong, but were quickly learning that so much depended on factors out of their control. Just two years in, they were struggling.

Gordon watched as Russ started rubbing his hands together as he did when he was stressed and thinking hard. Gordon always had a calmer demeanor and was usually the one with a positive perspective, whereas Russ often took the worst-case-scenario angle. But Russ had been working the books. He had the education for the finances and had put the time in, double-checking, triple checking their numbers. Gordon trusted him in this but held out hope. "We just need more time," said Gordon. "Things will improve."

Russ stopped in front of the window and looked across the street at their service station, shaking his head. Gordon held his breath, pushing away the thought that this was the beginning of the end of his time as an American businessman. Just eight months ago it had seemed that money came easily to everyone. People were going places, they were buying, selling, spending, then suddenly it all halted. Gordon remembered hearing of his dad's short stint in the restaurant business—his "failed attempt at business," as he told them. He knew there was always the risk of failure, but so soon?

"I think we need to let the service station go," said Russ, still looking across the street. "We can keep the coal business, but we just can't afford to run both, and the way things are now, coal is the better business. If we let go of one, we have a better shot at keeping the other going."

Gordon let out his breath and let hope back in. He loved the service station, but he loved being a business owner more.

"Well, I guess if that would give us the best chance to survive, that's what we need to do." Gordon was a reasonable man and didn't like to argue. He knew Russ was correct, and they couldn't keep both. If they were to survive, they needed to put all their energy into one business. They needed to focus their attention, instead of dividing it. Selling the service station would give them a bit of a financial cushion as well. It was the right thing to do, even if it hurt to give it up. It was the most viable solution to keep failure out of the conversation. There was really no time to dwell on what they knew needed to be done. In the spring of 1931, Gordon and Russ kept as many employees as they could afford and sold the service station.

Like so much of life during those times, going through the process felt like driving through a tunnel in the dark. Gordon could only see a few feet in front of him, only what his headlights would illuminate. Everything around him was dark and seemed to be getting darker. Their future was so uncertain. But still, together they were moving forward. At least now they could move slightly more confidently, focusing on the one business that had hope. No one knew when the recession would end, or how, or if it would end, or if they would still be in business when it ended. But for now, they had family and hope—both of which they could lean on.

CHAPTER SIX

1932–1939

Success is not final, failure is not fatal
it is the courage to continue that counts.
—WINSTON CHURCHILL

BY THE FALL OF 1932, THE EFFECTS OF THE RECESSION WERE NOW widespread in Seattle. In fact, it was no longer a recession—the city was deep into the Great Depression. One in three people were unemployed. The Bon Marché no longer expected to top its sales from the previous Christmas. The outlook was so bleak that even those who still had money considered it a gift just to have breakfast on any given day. Many of the Clark brothers' previous customers had already decided not to buy coal this year. They were living day to day, just hoping to keep a roof over their heads.

Gordon and Russ knew their business on shaky ground. The residential coal industry was dependent on two things: winter temperatures (the colder the better), and people's ability to buy coal. Both factors were out of their control, but despite everything, they were better off than most. They still had the business, and they did have some customers. Selling the service station had given them so much relief. Now they could put all their efforts into the coal business.

Behind his red oak desk, Russ leaned back in his chair and looked toward the door that opened up onto Genesee Street. "We can't afford to lose many more customers," he said.

Gordon nodded and sighed. "We just have to hope the ones we have can pay." Over the past few years the brothers had run ads in the *Rainier Valley Times* that promised "Quality Service and Quality Fuel." They couldn't afford to pay for those ads anymore, but they hoped that those people who *could* buy coal would remember them and buy from Genesee Coal & Stoker.

"*If* we have any customers this year." Russ put his elbows on his desk and his hands on his head. Both brothers worried plenty, but Russ tended to do so outwardly, whereas Gordon kept his feelings in, worrying in his own quiet manner. Russ abruptly stood up. "We're nothing without customers. If we lose them, we lose everything." The reality was, it didn't matter how stellar their customer service was; if the customers didn't have money to pay, they just couldn't pay.

Gordon and Russ had watched customers they knew well lose their jobs and struggle. Then they'd watched them move out of foreclosed homes and into who-knows-where: likely the shantytown on the old tide flats of the Seattle shipyards called Hooverville, its name based on the general consensus that President Hoover had contributed to the instability and drastic fall of the economy. People leaving homes behind took with them whatever they could carry. They made shelters out of scrap metal, wood, or cardboard, and used anything they could find to stoke their meager fires, just trying to make it through the dismal winter one day at a time.

Each time he saw another family move out, Gordon gave silent gratitude for his job, home, and family. He knew it could soon be him. It was hard to watch this happen to anyone, but Gordon and Russ had gotten to know these people. They lived in the same neighborhood and said hello as they passed on the sidewalks. These were more than their customers. These were friends.

Then in March of 1933, just as it felt the whole country had hit rock bottom, the United States swore in a new president. People were desperate for a change, and Franklin D. Roosevelt arrived with a voice of hope. People in all corners of the country held on to his every word as transported via radio waves into their living rooms.

"First of all," the president said with a calm confidence, "let me assert my firm belief that the only thing we have to fear is fear itself." The inaugural speech continued. Roosevelt went on to promise that the dark realities of the day would disappear and soon be replaced by America's former state of success.

As he spoke, people remembered with fondness the prosperity they had once known. It hadn't been so long ago. They remembered those good times and held on to hope they would return. For some, that hope was the only thing they had. After that speech, President Roosevelt got right to work on his promises. He began restructuring the American banking system, assuring people that their money would be safer in these banks than under their mattresses.

In October 1933, booze started openly flowing as Prohibition was repealed in Washington State. Ray, now twenty-two, was still living with Si and Gordon. Even though Prohibition had been in effect since his arrival in Seattle, he somehow had returned to the juice that had gotten him into trouble as a teenager in Canada. But like Gordon and Russ, he was one of those fortunate enough to still have a job at the Port of Seattle. He seemed to be managing his habit better now than he had in Canada, so his family just let him be.

For those still without jobs and living in Hooverville, their hope might have been quickly washed away along with their cardboard walls when, in the fall of 1933, Seattle had record-breaking rains. The rain that season was relentless. It flooded the streets of downtown Seattle. Surrounding rivers overflowed, and homes on bluffs such as Leschi slid into the adjacent Lake Washington.

Month by month the weather was unpredictable, and so were Gordon and Russ's regular customers. The brothers were barely able to pay their employees, their bills, and themselves. In fact, sometimes they had to make sacrifices. The employees came first. Gordon and Russ couldn't run the company without them, and their workers, while lucky to have jobs at all, still really needed their pay. They all had families to feed.

Gordon and Russ stretched each dollar as far as they could and left the bills unpaid for as long as they could, until one day they received a letter from the phone company. If they didn't pay up, the company would disconnect their phones. That month, Gordon and Russ paid the phone bill, and not themselves. That approach, however, could not continue, or they'd soon find themselves in Hooverville, too.

As the dark days continued, Gordon found a bit of brightness on the steps of his apartment building. He looked forward to walking up and down the external hallways, hoping for a glimpse of—and perhaps a small conversation with—the pretty new Canadian neighbor, whose name was Katie.

"Nice day for a walk," said Gordon as he nodded and moved aside to let Katie down the stairs first.

"Oh, sure it is. That your car parked out there?" Katie seemed curious about Gordon as well. He always liked to engage in conversation about his car. Perhaps the three-piece suit he wore also impressed her.

"Yes, it is. Do you need a ride somewhere?" Gordon was always happy to help a neighbor, but he was extra happy to help this one.

"Oh no, I just wondered is all. It's a nice day for a walk. I don't have far to go."

Gordon chatted with her whenever he could, and eventually learned that Katie McLellan had moved from Winnipeg, Manitoba, and lived in the apartment with her younger sister, Agnes. Like many single women of her age at the time, Katie had moved to the city in order to find independence from her father's house.

Gordon was attracted to the way Katie seemed to look after her sister, but she was also beautiful. Her facial features were perfectly proportioned, and her blue eyes sparkled when she smiled. He most often saw her in her maid uniform—a modest blue dress with white-cuffed short sleeves, a white apron, and a lacy white collar around the neck. But on occasion he saw her on Sunday, on her way to church. Her Sunday dress hung long enough to cover her knees, and her felt cloche hat fit neatly, covering all but a small amount of her wavy, light-brown hair. She had a well-dressed yet humble look about her that Gordon liked.

Katie was the second-oldest girl of ten children. Her oldest sister, Florence, had already married and moved to the Ballard neighborhood of Seattle when their mother passed away. It was then, at age twelve, that Katie assumed the role of mother, caretaker of the house, and protector of her younger siblings. They all feared their father's temper, mood swings, and alcohol abuse, living each day grateful for the next. One by one, as the siblings became old enough to marry or move out, they did.

When her youngest sister Lola became pregnant out of wedlock, Katie and Agnes, the only remaining siblings in the house, left Winnipeg to take Lola to Vancouver, Canada, where another married sister lived. After Lola gave birth and gave the child up for adoption, she stayed in Vancouver, while Katie, now thirty, and Agnes moved to Seattle to start their lives far away from their unpredictable father and his inconsistent affection.

But since Katie's education had been interrupted in the sixth grade to care for her siblings, her only option for employment was what she knew how to do—even though she didn't particularly enjoy it—housekeeping. With the help of her older sister Florence, Katie was able to get a job with a family in the well-to-do Mount Baker neighborhood, close to her apartment in Rainier Valley.

To Katie, faith in God was the most important thing. It was her deep faith that had gotten her through the dark days under her father's roof. She had grown to believe God was her only protector—the only source she could depend on. She gave thanks before every meal, and never missed church on Sunday. In her mind, there was no gray area. Either you were a saved Christian, or you were not. To Katie it was black and white—right or wrong, good or bad, sin or not a sin. Gordon liked that simplicity.

In getting to know Katie, Gordon rekindled his own faith. Back in Leduc, the family attended church on Sunday, but Annie had been the driver in getting them to go. Once she was gone, their regular attendance went as well. They always claimed to be Presbyterian, and once in Seattle, they would call Mount Baker Park Presbyterian their church, but never actually became part of the congregation.

Now, throughout their courtship, Gordon started attending Katie's church, Hope Gospel Hall in north Seattle. Over time, Gordon grew to understand how Katie's faith gave her an unconditional sense of security. Gordon sensed she was growing more and more secure in their relationship as well. He enjoyed being in the role of confidant and found satisfaction in feeling needed and trusted.

Just as the "New Deal" economy started to turn up slightly, in March 1935, Gordon felt financially secure enough to marry Katie and move into a rental house of their own. Soon after, Ray married as well. Although they were all relieved that Ray seemed to have settled down, there was something about his marriage to Hazel that had Si shaking his head. "That marriage will never last," Si would mutter to Gordon and Katie. Hazel liked to have a good time, and brought out the party in Ray. She was like a younger, more spontaneous version of Russ's wife Beulah, but without the education and the work ethic—a combination that concerned Si. But Ray made his choice, and now that all three boys were married and living in their own houses, Si rotated living among the three.

Although the brothers' romantic lives were moving forward at a steady pace, business was still merely limping along. Gordon and Russ had continued to run the business with an emphasis on customer service. They genuinely cared for their neighbors and wanted to help those who were struggling to heat their homes—and plenty of customers were—as the economy into 1936 was soft at best. This meant providing fuel to some who couldn't pay right away. Acting on good faith, the brothers allowed loyal customers the flexibility to pay when they could. Of course, this put pressure on the business. Gordon and Russ were in a conundrum, trying very hard to keep customers for the future, while still being able to pay their employees and overhead expenses.

In late spring 1936, Gordon especially felt the crunch. On his way home from work one evening, a police officer followed him right into his driveway, told him to slow down, and wrote him a ticket. Gordon had a heavy foot, and the ticket was a hefty one. After paying, Gordon didn't have any money left to bring home that week. It wasn't a good time to be flat broke. Katie was just a few weeks away from giving birth to their first and—as it turned out—their only baby.

Donald Silas Clark was born June 9, 1936. Gordon was immediately smitten with Donnie, but Katie suffered the "baby blues." Within weeks of his birth, she became overwhelmed with anxiety and fear. For every tiny change in Donnie's behavior, she worried that something was wrong—that he was sick, or that she was doing something incorrectly. She immediately started questioning her worth as a mother and began fearing things that were out of her control. It was a side of Katie that Gordon hadn't seen, and he wondered if her stolen childhood was resurfacing.

Then the pendulum swung the other direction. While chaos ensued inside Gordon's personal life, the economy finally stabilized and began improving. By the end of 1936, more customers were paying than not; by 1938, the economy was showing signs of a true resurgence.

Genesee Coal & Stoker was now consistently making enough money in the winter to carry it through the summer, and Gordon and Russ were able to save on top of that. The housing market had even picked up. Gordon and Katie, needing more room, were able to seize the opportunity and bought a house on Carver Street in Rainier Beach for $3,000.

The three-bedroom, two-story house with both a front

yard and a backyard had just the right amount of space. Just a few blocks up from the water and about four miles from the office, it was the perfect location. The new house even had room enough for Si. Gordon and Katie had been hoping for another child to fill the extra bedroom, but because so far they had only been blessed with one, Si took the spare bedroom and called the house on Carver Street his permanent address.

Si adored his new role as grandfather, although he didn't like to make a fuss in front of anyone. In a crowd, he acted as if Donnie's presence was nothing special, but when no one else was looking, he fussed over the baby as only a lovesick grandfather can do.

Donnie wasn't the only one who benefitted from Si's presence. Gordon noticed Katie also seemed to be in a better mental state when Si was around. She showed a tremendous respect for her father-in-law. To her he was a genuine, caring, true father figure—one who didn't yell at or belittle his children, causing them to question their value and deservingness of even God's love, but rather gave unconditional love and approval. Si was the opposite of her own father, whom she described as a tyrant. He was the father she'd always needed.

Although he considered his home to be with Gordon and Katie on Carver Street, Si periodically visited Ray and Hazel in Grotto, Washington. Grotto was a sparsely populated town northeast of Seattle. The small but growing town, surrounded by trees, near a river, and situated just off the train route appealed to Si. It brought him back to his early days in Leduc with Annie.

Si got along fine with Hazel, but she and Ray fought like dogs after the same bone. Ray continued to drink and now worked in the timber industry, having lost his job at the Port of Seattle. Si never stayed long in Grotto—just a night or two at a time, but June 23, 1939 would be his last. On that night, while in Grotto, Si passed away peacefully in his sleep. His heart simply stopped. He was 76 years old.

In the ten years since his immigration, Si had made quite a positive impression on everyone he met, as was evident in the numerous cards and flowers both Gordon and Russ received after his passing. "Your father will be deeply missed" and "I will miss his kind heart and warm smile" were just a few of the sentiments expressed. Struggling to accept their father's death, Gordon and Russ had to quickly move through their grief so they could face another reality that was starting to threaten the business. Residential heating trends were shifting. The economy had been slowly climbing as the Depression ended, and along with that growth came more choices in heating fuels.

Previously, Gordon and Russ had worried about losing customers to Hooverville. Now that finances had stabilized, customers were leaving for a new reason. It wasn't because they couldn't afford to buy coal, but because they were switching to a new, popular trend in residential heating: oil burners.

Coal was becoming a dirty word in more ways than one. Heating oil was a new product and cleaner burning than coal. After a season of heating with coal, customers had to beat the soot out of their carpets or wipe off the fine layer of black dust left on every horizontal surface. Now, new heating oil companies were popping up, right in Gordon and Russ's neighborhood, and stealing business at a rate the brothers feared would end them.

At first, Gordon and Russ thought they had no recourse. Oil was a different fuel, and they provided coal. They briefly thought that maybe they'd dropped the wrong company when they decided to let the service station go. Service stations were still in business as car sales had picked up. They hadn't seen this coming. Who could have predicted that a new source of fuel could squeeze Genesee Coal & Stoker out of business?

"We could add oil to our business," suggested Gordon.

"We don't know anything about heating oil. We'd have to buy a truck." Russ usually didn't like Gordon's ideas right off the bat.

"Well, if we add oil, we could at least keep the customers who want to switch from coal to oil." Gordon had a child now, and Katie wanted another. He couldn't afford to have any more desperate times when he didn't get paid.

Russ felt a little more comfortable with the situation, since he didn't have children. He and Beulah enjoyed their social lives and felt that they didn't have space for the inconveniences children brought. They liked to go out to dinner, to parties, and on vacation whenever they pleased. They had a dog—a hunting dog—so Russ spent his weekends bird hunting. It also seemed that Russ didn't have the energy to start something new. "Nah, we'll still have plenty of coal customers. They won't all convert to oil. Will they?" The question hung in the air uncomfortably long.

CHAPTER SEVEN

1941–1945

Even if I knew that tomorrow the world would go to pieces,
I would still plant my apple tree.
—MARTIN LUTHER

AS IT TURNED OUT, RUSS WAS RIGHT—NOT EVERYONE SWITCHED to oil. Over the next few years, Genesee Coal & Stoker kept enough coal customers to maintain a good business. It wasn't growing, but they had built a solid reputation, and customers remained steady. Although Russ seemed just fine with this scenario, Gordon was still bothered. He was looking ahead at the bigger picture, and wondered about the future of coal.

Gordon looked at his son, just five years old, as they turned the corner from Carver Street to Waters Avenue. They were heading to the beach at Pritchard Island, which was no longer an actual island but a peninsula since Lake Washington had been lowered to cut the Ship Canal in 1917. Katie held Gordon's arm as they walked side by side a few steps behind Donnie on his tricycle.

It was a Saturday, the first warm, sunny day of spring after several months of gray clouds and drizzle. It was the kind of day in Seattle that lifted everyone's spirits. Abandoned bicycles littered the grass leading to the beach, and picnic blankets began to appear a few steps further. Kids ran splashing into the cold water.

Katie and Gordon watched as Donnie joined the fun—splashing and laughing, not a care in the world. Gordon envied the boy's carefree spirit. He assumed he'd had that same joyful temperament at that age. But he wondered how his parents had felt. Did Si have as much worry about the future and sustainability of the farm as Gordon now did about the business? Had his mother feared change while her sons were growing up as strongly as Katie did?

Gordon thought about how his father had built the farm not only to satisfy his own sense of accomplishment, but also with the intention of leaving it to his sons. Although it wasn't the same soil, the farm Si built had given Gordon and his brothers a start in life. His father had left him that legacy, and now he was building on it for his son. Genesee Coal & Stoker had done well and made it through a tough time. But Gordon was starting to wonder about its long-term survival. *Does this company have a future if we stick with coal?*

Over the next several months, Gordon and Russ were in opposite corners when it came to the idea of adding heating oil to their inventory. Their discussions went in circles. Russ wasn't budging, and Gordon wasn't ready to put the topic to rest. But any discussions about the future of the business were diverted on December 7, 1941, when the bombing of Pearl Harbor launched the United States into World War II. Just like when they'd learned of the stock market crash in 1929, the brothers didn't know how this news would affect the company. But one thing was certain: now was not the time for big changes.

At the United States' entry into the war, Gordon and Russ felt pretty secure, and thankful that they would not be called to serve. The age groups initially required to register for the draft were twenty-one to thirty-six. Gordon and Russ were just barely too old; Ray, however, at age thirty, was not.

More than a decade had passed since Gordon, Si, and Ray had stood in front of Annie's grave in Canada and said good-bye. Since then, while living, eating, breathing, and working in America, they'd become American citizens, and begun to view Canada as their birthplace and the site of their childhood but not their home.

Uncle Sam's famous finger pointed right at Ray: "I want YOU for the U.S. Army." Those posters, originally created for World War I, were quickly resurrected and landed on sidewalks and in storefront windows around Seattle. If Ray had had a good reason to defer, he wouldn't have done so. He had no reason not to fight for his country. It was his patriotic duty. Given his age, his single status (he and Hazel had recently divorced), and the fact that he didn't have children, he was a prime candidate. Just a few months later, Ray headed to Fort Lewis, just south of Tacoma, Washington, for basic training.

Visitation day at Fort Lewis couldn't come soon enough. Gordon was anxious to see how Ray was getting along, and he also thought the trip would be a good outing for Donnie. At age six, the boy constantly played with his combat airplane, military truck, and miniature toy soldiers. But when the day came, and the armed guards closed and locked the tall gate topped with coiled barbed wire behind the visitors, Donnie burst into tears, thinking they were locked in for good. Suddenly wartime had become very real.

The moment Gordon saw his younger brother at Fort Lewis, he felt a heaviness he hadn't felt in years. After their mother died and Si became crippled with grief, Gordon had taken on a parenting role with Ray. Now that Si was gone, he felt once again the weight of responsibility. He tried to put on a confident show.

"Looking sharp in that uniform, kid." Gordon's instincts told him to keep his younger brother away from danger, but he also felt a sense of pride. Ray stood tall, nodded at Gordon, then briefly rubbed Donnie's head, messing up his hair a bit before giving him a couple firm pats.

"You like my uniform, too?" he said to Donnie. Ray tended to seek diversion in order to avoid emotional situations. There was nervous tension in the moment, and it seemed everyone wanted to keep the mood light. But Gordon saw the look in Ray's eyes. He knew his brother was touched they were there.

"I sure do, Uncle Ray. And your shiny shoes," said Donnie, as Katie laughed out loud and shook her head.

"Always noticing shoes, just like your father," she said.

Gordon knew this was also Katie's way of managing her emotions. Talk of the war added to her list of things to worry about. She was visibly anxious seeing Ray in uniform, knowing the reality of what that meant. The whole country lay under a heavy blanket of seriousness. Gordon felt it, too, though he tried to suppress it. Leaving the fort that day, he told himself over and over that Ray would be fine.

Meanwhile, civilians were repeating the slogan "We're all in this together," an attempt to keep a positive attitude even though families had been torn apart. Wanting to do his part and to keep his own family safe, Gordon volunteered to be an air raid warden in his Rainier Beach neighborhood. Air raid wardens were issued the same helmets as those worn by the soldiers, with small holes drilled into the rim to differentiate them from those intended for the men in the trenches.

On nights when blackouts were in effect, Gordon put on his helmet, marked with a large block letter "W" for warden, and walked around Rainier Beach. He made sure porch lights were out and blackout blinds pulled, so no glimmer of light could attract an enemy plane if one entered the airspace. On occasion, in the eerily dark and quiet streets, he had to remind a neighbor of the potential fine for leaving an outside light on.

To Gordon, this was an important job and worth doing. Boeing was building planes in Seattle, so an enemy attack was a possibility they had to prepare for. With his brother at war, Gordon wanted to contribute by protecting the neighborhood. Katie, however, was becoming increasingly fearful. She didn't want to talk about war and enemy air raids, but every time Gordon wore his helmet, it was a visible reminder of the threat that lurked right outside the door. So, Katie retreated inward.

As the United States entered the war, manufacturing assembly lines quickly transitioned from building cars to building planes. In fact, the changeover happened so abruptly, some not-quite-complete cars came out with wooden bumpers instead of steel ones. Seeing those odd-looking cars on the road, Gordon felt pretty good about his gray 1939 Buick. It was the first of its kind, with a flashing turn signal: a tiny switch on the gearshift mounted to the steering column.

On weeknights just before dinner, Donnie often ran to the corner of Waters Avenue and Carver Street to meet Gordon. The boy cherished the time with his dad and couldn't wait for him to arrive home from work. Upon his first glimpse of the Buick, Donnie would start jumping up and down, waving frantically until the Buick stopped to pick him up.

"Well, hello there, son." Gordon opened the driver's side door. "You want to drive?"

Donnie climbed onto his lap behind the wheel. "Is it time for the turn signal, Dad?" Like his father, Donnie had already developed a passion for cars. He loved helping his dad wash the Buick, and he especially loved how it looked when it was all clean.

By December 1942, anyone who owned a car understood they had to keep their tires in good shape "for the duration," meaning until the war was over. Tires and gasoline were now heavily rationed. Japan had seized the rubber-producing countries and cut off supply to the United States.

In order to monitor and limit gasoline usage, the government issued ration stickers to all car owners. The stickers were visibly displayed in the lower right corner of the front windshield, each with a boldface typed letter. The A, for the general public, entitled the holder of the sticker to four gallons of gasoline per week. A green sticker with a white B was issued to business owners and allowed them eight gallons per week. Even better than the green B sticker was the black sticker with a white X. These were given to police officers, firemen, and anyone dependent on their vehicle to provide comfort and safety to civilians. Gordon and Russ once again found themselves among the few and fortunate. Providing heat, and therefore comfort, during the cold, dark days of winter entitled Genesee Coal & Stoker to the black sticker with the white X, and unlimited gasoline and tires.

If during the Depression it had felt as though nothing could go their way, during the war the brothers seemed to be catching all the breaks. Many men of prime working age from the heating industry had closed up shop and gone off to war. Suddenly, Gordon and Russ's prewar competition had disappeared. They were among the few working-age men lucky to be left at home to run their businesses. With less competition, and over the course of another cold winter, Genesee Coal & Stoker's customer base grew significantly.

Adding to their advantages was a new pricing policy for heating fuel. During the war, the Office of Price Administration controlled the prices for all things, including coal. This cap on the price of coal actually helped Genesee Coal & Stoker during that time. Knowing that prices wouldn't change, people ordered coal confidently. They also paid their bills without question.

The war was all anyone talked about, thought about, and heard about. No one knew what the next day's news would bring. Fearing the worst, people tended either to spring into action or shut down with angst. For some women, fear made them act. Boeing's production of planes skyrocketed in factories largely staffed by women, since so many men had gone to join the military. But for a mother who already worried about everything under the sun, the fear brought on by the war didn't put Katie to work—it tipped her toward depression.

Gordon tried to stay positive and productive, both for the good of the country and for the good of the family. Alongside his work as an air raid warden, he planted a victory garden and busied himself with projects around the house. Gordon was proud of how Donnie helped, too. Donnie always wanted to please his parents. He seemed to like being given the responsibility for important tasks. He jumped at the opportunity to take the ration book to the store to buy the family's weekly allotment of sugar and meat.

On one occasion, though, when he arrived home from a trip to the store and handed over the provisions to his mother, he couldn't find the ration book.

"What do you mean you haven't got the book?" Katie questioned. Donnie dug deep in his pockets again, then turned and ran out the door to retrace his steps. Gordon held his breath while Katie recounted the event later that night, knowing it must have been stressful for both of them, then smiled with relief to learn that the book had been found lying in the center of the sidewalk, where it had fallen out of Donnie's pocket.

By spring of 1945, it seemed the war had gone on and on. *For the duration* was feeling more like *forever*. But attitudes continued to be patriotic. People had gotten used to rationing, growing their own vegetables, and sharing a ride, though luxury items such as toys, nicer clothing, cars, and bikes were getting old and run-down. Even if a person had the money to buy them, those items just weren't available for purchase during the war. The only things being made on assembly lines were necessities and goods for the troops.

This fact frustrated Gordon as Donnie's birthday approached. The boy had wanted a bike for a while now, but Katie had insisted he wait until he was nine years old. Now that the day was coming, Gordon wanted to deliver on that promise. But since the bike couldn't be a brand-new one, he would have to make a used one look brand-new.

Typically resourceful, Gordon found a customer whose child had outgrown his bike. It was the perfect size for Donnie. After paying a fair price for the dilapidated bike, Gordon brought it into his shop behind Genesee Coal & Stoker and took the whole thing apart. At his workbench, he cleaned and greased every part, replaced the ones he could, and put on new tires. He then put the bike back together again and painted it bright red. By the time he finished, it was perfect.

Donnie was quite possibly the happiest kid on the block that day in June. Gordon looked at Katie as she smiled and gave a little chuckle, watching Donnie's excitement. In that moment he saw the independent, secure, caring woman he had fallen in love with. She looked brighter and more cheerful.

Maybe she just needed something new, bright, and shiny to smile about, Gordon thought. Maybe they all did.

Soon the whole country did have something to smile about. Just as abruptly as it had begun, in September 1945, the war ended. The news brought joy to everyone. Storeowners ran to their doors and shouted with delight, people honked car horns, and schoolchildren leapt out of their seats. There was a nationwide feeling of elation and triumph.

Shortly after that, the troops came home, including Ray. Gordon was relieved, and even Katie stood a little taller when she saw Ray safely returned. Feeling proud to be an American, Ray went back to work in the industry that had grounded him in his first months in the United States. As a teenager, he had worked as a dockhand at the Port of Seattle. Now he returned to work at Fisherman's Terminal—not as a dockhand, but as a fish broker. In this capacity, Ray was the negotiator between fishermen and retail buyers. He enjoyed the new job, which was one he had aspired to as a youngster just starting out at the Port.

For everyone, visions of the American dream became as tangible as Frederick & Nelson's storefront displays in downtown Seattle. Big-ticket items that had been so scarce during the war suddenly became available and were acquired by many. But amidst the euphoria hovered a cloud of cynicism, and hard transitions followed.

Veterans came home needing work, and, having lost military contracts overnight, thousands of Boeing and local shipyard employees lost their jobs. People craved prosperity, but the end of the war brought change that wasn't easy for many. Although Gordon and Russ were once again among the most fortunate, still maintaining a business and even holding savings in the bank, Genesee Coal & Stoker wasn't exempt from the difficult phase that was beginning.

Initially, the brothers thought the postwar spending spree promised an even better heating season. But Genesee was still only serving up coal, and coal as a heat source was falling rapidly out of style. Modern oil furnaces were the fast-growing trend. Everything about oil was cleaner than coal, but the main attraction was that it didn't leave a fine layer of soot on surfaces inside the home. People who'd had money during the war and no place to use it now felt a desire to spend. Many decided it was time at last to upgrade to an oil furnace. As Genesee Coal & Stoker started to lose customers, Gordon and Russ revisited the old argument.

"Who knows what kind of problems adding oil to the business would bring?" commented Russ. He hadn't changed his tune. He was just plain stubborn.

But Gordon liked the idea of purveying the newest and the best. "If oil is the best, it's what we should be providing our customers." He wasn't planning on backing down this time. They needed to add heating oil if they were going to stay in the game. "We have the money. Might as well buy a new oil truck." Russ, Gordon knew, also had a soft spot for cars and trucks.

Finally, Gordon succeeded. In the spring of 1946, Genesee Coal & Stoker bought an oil truck and signed a heating oil supply contract with the Time Oil Company. Just as the end of the war had given Americans something to cheer about, the addition of heating oil to the business invigorated Gordon and Russ as well.

Though Russ had been slow to get on board, once he did, he quickly got excited about steering the company in a new direction. But the change meant even more to Gordon. He saw that the company now had a better chance at longevity. They were adding value, and possibly building a legacy to pass on to the next generation. Gordon smiled inside knowing his dad, Si, would also have been pleased.

CHAPTER EIGHT

1946–1949

Opportunity is missed by most people because it is dressed in
overalls and looks like work.
—THOMAS EDISON

GORDON THOUGHT THE SHINY NEW RED OIL TRUCK PARKED
behind the Genesee Coal & Stoker building looked worthy of a
few photos. Since the end of the war, money had been burning
a hole in Gordon's pocket. Now that luxury items were available
to buy, Gordon had spared no expense in purchasing the
best camera on the shelves: a Kodak 35, the top of the line.
Gordon and Russ took turns posing proudly in front of their
brand-new 1,200-gallon Chevrolet oil truck while the other
snapped a shot.

As exciting as it was to expand their offerings, it had also
brought on mountains of work learning the oil side of business.
Instead of changing their name to accommodate oil in
addition to coal, they decided to create a "Burner Oil Department."
Later, when their oil sales started to overtake
their sales of coal, they would change the name to Genesee

Fuel Company, allowing them to market themselves more efficiently.

Although at first Russ was skeptical about whether this oil business was really necessary, he quickly changed his tune. The brothers had signed a contract with Time Oil, making Time their exclusive supplier and allowing them the best wholesale price. Since Russ was the more experienced businessman, it was his job to deal with the suppliers while Gordon communicated with the customers. It didn't take long for Russ to realize that entering into this relationship with Time put him at an elevated level. Suddenly he wasn't just an independent local fuel company owner. He was now rubbing elbows with heavy hitters in the oil business.

While work at the office had gotten busier and more challenging, life at home was feeling less stressful for Gordon. Katie was physically and emotionally relieved the war was over. Her worried brow had relaxed, her smile returned. Now that blackouts were a thing of the past, Donnie was allowed to spend summer evenings after dinner at the Rainier Beach Playfield, playing pickup games of baseball with his pack of regulars.

Ten-year-old Donnie was even crazier for baseball now. He was the first generation in the family born in the United States. Among the Clarks, there seemed to be a direct correlation between interest in the classic American sport and the age at which it was introduced. Of the three Clark brothers, Ray was the most interested. But not having had the opportunity to play baseball as a boy in Canada, he had significantly less passion for the sport than Donnie, who'd learned it on the playground at school.

Professional baseball had largely gone dormant during the war, but now that the focus was no longer on the activity overseas, the way was paved for a return of interest. Fresh energy revived the classic American sport in Seattle. The original Dugdale Park Stadium, the one that had caught Ray's eye on his first trip down Rainier Avenue, had tragically burned to the ground in 1932.

In 1938, Emil Sick, who owned the iconic Rainier Beer brewery, bought the Pacific Coast League's Seattle Indians and renamed them the Seattle Rainiers. He then built a new stadium on the same site as the old Dugdale Park Stadium, and called it Sick's Stadium. For Seattle area baseball fans in the postwar years, Sick's Stadium was the place to be.

Amidst the renewed baseball fever, Donnie relished any opportunity to watch the Seattle Rainiers at the nearby stadium, always bringing his glove in hopes of catching a foul ball. Better yet, he also always hoped to get an autograph from Jo Jo White or "Kewpie" Dick Barrett. When he couldn't watch from inside the stadium, he watched from the front porch of his Uncle Russ and Aunt Beulah's new house, which sat on the hill above Vacca Farms and had a free, unobstructed view of the outfield.

Yearly visits by "Old Woody" to the Rainier Beach Playfield drew the biggest crowd of baseball-loving kids. The popular *Seattle Times*-sponsored kids' pitching contest employed the use of a rectangular, wood-faced frame with a hole cut out to resemble a strike zone. Donnie and his friends gathered around to watch as each kid got a chance to pitch to imaginary batters behind this frame, called "Old Woody." If three pitches went through the hole before four pitched balls missed the target, the batter struck out, and the pitching contestant went on to face the next imaginary batter.

Summers in Seattle, especially after the war, and specifically in Rainier Beach, were idyllic for Donnie. As September approached, the days got shorter, while temperatures often got hotter. Sometime in mid-October, Seattle tended to make an abrupt transition from an extended Indian summer to the cool temperatures of fall. The end of warm weather meant the end of baseball season. Cold overnight temperatures awakened hibernating furnaces, and the heating season began.

One Saturday in mid-October, Donnie was throwing a ball way up high and catching it in his glove while Gordon tended to his garden. The phone rang inside, and, although Katie was there to answer, Gordon instinctively put down his gardening tools and headed inside. The sunshine had been warming things up, but temperatures had been colder than usual overnight. Gordon had a feeling he knew what that phone call was about. Donnie did, too. His dad was busier during the cold weather. Even on weekends Gordon was busy making house calls, kick-starting furnaces that wouldn't fire up on their own.

Gordon's customers knew that if they had a problem with their furnace outside regular business hours, they could call him at home. Listening to one side of the telephone conversation, Donnie knew exactly what would happen next.

When Gordon hung up the phone, he headed straight to his bedroom. This was a routine familiar to Donnie as he waited for his dad to come out in his three-piece suit, ready for work, even on a Saturday. For Gordon, looking sharp was necessary for a good businessman, regardless of the day, the time, or the status of the customer. His Fahey-Brockman had held up pretty well while threads were scarce during the war, but Gordon thought it might be time for a new one—a modern oilman needed to indulge in a new suit at the high end: Littler's this time.

Once he was ready, Gordon picked up his flashlight and his electrical current tester. "Donnie, I gotta go take a look at the old doctor's furnace. You wanna come?"

"Well, sure I wanna come." Donnie grabbed his glove and ball before following his dad out the door.

Donnie loved going with his dad on house calls. He was proud of his dad and liked the idea of being a businessman's assistant. This particular call was more exciting than most, since the old doctor's son was a local hero—the great Fred Hutchinson. Fred was now playing in the big leagues, as a pitcher for the Detroit Tigers.

By this time, Dr. Joseph Hutchinson, "the old doctor," was the most well-respected doctor in south Seattle. In the early 1900s, Dr. Hutchinson had done everything from performing surgeries to delivering babies. He made house calls via horse and buggy, and also by boat to the south end of Mercer Island before roads made it more accessible. He was the kind of doctor who, if his patients couldn't afford to pay him, would accept whatever they could give: produce from their garden, eggs, baked goods. He was Gordon's doctor and also one of his loyal customers. By the mid-'40s, he had a storefront office in Rainier Beach, but he still saw his patients most often by making house calls, just as Gordon was doing now.

The Hutchinsons' three-story Victorian house stood proud on the corner, with a well-manicured yard and detail-painted window trim. Donnie and Gordon walked up the wooden steps and rang the doorbell. Much to their surprise, when the door opened, instead of being greeted by the old doctor or Mrs. Hutchinson, they saw, standing taller than life, the great Fred Hutchinson himself.

Hutch, as he was called, had grown up holding a ball and glove, playing pickup games on the Rainier Beach Playfields, same as Donnie. The neighborhood boys were always comparing themselves to and dreaming about being like Hutch. When it seemed as if Old Woody could never be beaten, Donnie and his friends would console each other by saying, "Don't worry, Hutch probably couldn't even beat Old Woody," although of course, he probably had.

"Well, hello there, Fred." Gordon spoke as if he and Hutch were old friends. "This is my boy here. He's a ballplayer, too."

Donnie, only as tall as Fred's belt buckle, held on to his glove and looked up at his hero. His jaw dropped open a little as if he was ready to speak, but nothing came out. Fred wore casual clothes and a baseball cap.

"Hello. Nice to meet you," said Fred simply, with a nod. Too stunned to know what to do, Donnie only bit his bottom lip and said nothing. Gordon then filled the void.

"Is the old doctor in? He wanted me to take a look at his furnace."

Fred opened the door and led Gordon and Donnie down to the basement where the old coal furnace stood useless. Not wasting time, Gordon took out his flashlight and got to work. Donnie stood awestruck, not able to be of much help in that moment. He thought about Old Woody and wondered how many times Hutch had won that contest. He also wondered what the kids at the playfield would say when he told them he had come face-to-face with the pitcher for the Detroit Tigers.

Gordon, in his three-piece suit, with just his flashlight and his electric current finder, got the old doctor's furnace working that day. It was an easy fix; otherwise he would have called in one of his furnace technicians. Meeting Fred Hutchinson on his doorstep that day was unquestionably a highlight for Donnie. In 1946, Hutch was a homegrown major-league base-ball hero. Donnie would never have imagined that decades later, the name Fred Hutchinson would more often be associ-ated with cancer research than baseball. Fred's older brother, Dr. William Hutchinson, founded the Fred Hutchinson Cancer Research Center in 1975, naming it after his brother, the base-ball hero who fell victim to cancer in 1964.

For Gordon, house calls like that were business as usual.

But they were also another example of how Gordon's character and values were reflected in his business. He'd drop everything to help a neighbor. He treated customers like family. He valued his community. Genesee had taken a risk in buying an oil truck and expanding its services, but for Gordon, it was a risk worth taking if it meant longevity for the business.

It was also on house calls such as these—especially when Donnie came along—that Gordon felt nostalgia for his dad. Leduc had been on his mind lately because he had recently received word from his Canadian relatives. They'd written to report that oil rigs on farmland outside Leduc, very near Si's old property, had hit a mother lode of crude oil.

How ironic, thought Gordon. Another cousin had sent him a newspaper clipping that read "Farmer Strikes it Rich in Canada," along with a photo that took Gordon back in time. The farmer, his wife, and kids all wore simple clothing: overalls, boots, and hats appropriate for farming. Fond memories of his childhood on the farm in Leduc rose to the surface of Gordon's mind.

But just as quickly, the recent memory of Donnie accompanying him to the old doctor's house brought a feeling of relief. Looking at the newspaper photo, Gordon noticed that one of the farmer's children looked to be about Donnie's age. But that child probably didn't have a baseball glove or a shiny red bicycle, two things that had made Donnie so happy and Gordon pleased to provide.

More than a dozen times Gordon had wondered, *What if we hadn't sold the farm and moved to Seattle? What if I hadn't met*

John Scott just as he wanted to sell his service station? Now more than ever, he was sure that the initial decision he had made all those years ago, setting off the string of important events that followed, had been the right one, regardless of the fame Leduc was now receiving.

In the two years since Genesee Coal & Stoker added oil to its business, the brothers had made more coal-to-oil conversions than they'd ever thought possible. They still delivered coal to those customers who had coal furnaces, but that number was decreasing drastically and they were not gaining any new coal customers. It was time to officially change their name to Genesee Fuel & Heating.

Well into 1948, people in Seattle were still in a postwar celebratory mood. Money flowed as it hadn't done since before the stock market crash in 1929. One pastor friend of Gordon's noted that after the war, they didn't even need to hold a bake sale to raise money for the church. All they had to do, he said, was open their doors and people practically threw money in.

Luckily for Gordon and Russ, people were beginning to see furnace upgrades as a necessary home improvement. Soon, Genesee Fuel was installing oil burners and burying oil tanks underground so fast, they had to hire more people just to dig holes. Once a conversion was complete, it was as easy as flipping a switch—the homeowner's existing furnace heated with oil for fuel, instead of coal. As Gordon's and Russ's coal customers diminished, their oil customers grew.

While a growing company is always a good thing, it is never without growing pains. The coal yard, where the trucks filled up for deliveries, was on their property, but the oil storage facility was not. That meant that once a day, the Genesee Fuel truck had to make the hour-long commute to Tacoma to fill up at the Time Oil storage facility. Because Genesee had added so many oil customers, the brothers feared they would either need to buy another truck or find another solution. This, of course, was a good problem to have. But another problem meant another solution that would have to be agreed upon by both Gordon and Russ.

Gordon stood out back behind the office and looked at the empty space they used for a parking lot. Russ walked out the back door to find him standing there and gave him a quizzical look. "Russ," Gordon said, "what do you think about putting a couple oil storage tanks on our property?"

"Why would we do that when we can just go fill up at Time?" Russ didn't wait for Gordon's response before he walked away. After nearly twenty years in business with his brother, Gordon knew exactly what to do next. He knew he had to give Russ time to let that idea simmer, just as he had with other major business decisions, such as the one they'd made to buy the lot they were currently standing on.

That had been a disagreement, too. In 1930, when the economy was falling fast, the owner of the lot behind the Genesee Coal & Stoker office building had defaulted on his tax payments. That created the opportunity to buy the property at a low cost. Since they had the money, Gordon thought acquiring it might provide a future opportunity of some sort. Russ didn't agree. He didn't see any need for extra space then, but in the end, Gordon won him over. Standing on that lot now, Gordon proposed they use the space Russ had never really wanted for storage tanks that he didn't want, either.

It was a typical situation. Russ was satisfied with the way the company was maintaining, while Gordon wanted to grow it, to do more, to make it better. But by now Gordon knew his brother and business partner well. He knew he just had to let Russ be Russ and work it out in his own way.

Meanwhile, Gordon turned his attention to Donnie. Now thirteen, the boy had a job delivering the *Seattle Shopping News* on Thursdays. Since he had long since outgrown his red bicycle, he was delivering the papers on foot. Donnie had his eye on a new Schwinn, with knee-action spring, hand brakes, a light on the fender, and a built-in kickstand. Just like his dad, Donnie usually wanted the newest and the best of any product. He would put in the extra hours working and wait an extra month or two so that he would have just enough for the top model, which in this case cost $90.

Once finally on his Schwinn and in typical teenage fashion, Donnie liked to ride at full speed down Waters Avenue, arms spread like eagle wings. It was a vision that made Gordon cringe, but at the same time it warmed his heart to see Donnie so carefree and happy. It made him realize what an idyllic life this was for a boy. It was a long way from baling hay and milking cows.

Before Donnie got his job delivering the paper, he had

occasionally ridden on the new oil truck with one of the company's trusted drivers, Wayne. Donnie was eager to help mostly because at the end of the day, when Wayne stopped at the tavern for a drink before heading back to the office, he bought Donnie a candy bar. Although Donnie thought of this as his "job," Gordon saw it as more of a way to keep Donnie busy on a Saturday so that he didn't bother Katie, as she'd become more worrisome again and her ability to keep up with housework had started to slip.

Donnie's next job, at age fourteen, earned him fifty cents per hour. He rode along with Ed Campbell, Genesee's coal delivery driver. During home deliveries, while Ed shoveled the coal down the chute, it was Donnie's job to make sure all the pieces of coal collected evenly at the base of the furnace in the customer's basement. Donnie liked earning money. He liked feeling like a businessman, and he really liked talking to the customers. He always introduced himself as Don Clark, which is what everyone other than his family called him. Sometimes he even received tips and, from one customer, a homemade apple pie.

As oil conversions continued, the trips to South Seattle to fill oil trucks increased. It had gotten to the point where Genesee's drivers had to make the two-hour round-trip trek south on I-5 multiple times per day. Finally, just as Gordon predicted, in 1949 Russ got on board with installing two 12,000-gallon underground tanks beneath their empty lot. Instead of heading to Tacoma, the drivers filled up the company trucks right outside the office. It saved both time and gasoline. Since a 12-

inch thick slab of concrete on top allowed for driving on top of the tanks, Russ didn't even have to lose his favorite parking space.

Watching his delivery drivers return to the lot at the end of the day filled Gordon with a sense of satisfaction. Once again he thought back to Leduc, where he'd driven tractors, first with his dad and then on his own. He couldn't help but wonder whether Donnie would be on one of those trucks by himself someday.

CHAPTER NINE

1900–1902

*You cannot swim for new horizons until you have courage
to lose sight of the shore.*
—WILLIAM FAULKNER

WHILE CITY LIVING HAD BEEN ATTRACTIVE IN THE FIRST HALF OF
the century, the suburban neighborhoods outside Seattle had
become more popular after the war. Mercer Island sat a little
over a mile off Seattle in the middle of Lake Washington. Until
just before the war, access to Mercer Island was limited to a
ferry that ran from the Leschi neighborhood of Seattle to
Roanoke Landing on the island. Then in 1940, the world's
longest floating bridge was built across Lake Washington,
connecting Seattle to Mercer Island and encouraging further
growth of the suburbs there. Now new neighborhoods were
mushrooming, and people wanted all things modern—including new heating oil furnaces.

In his mid-forties now, Gordon was feeling pretty good
about the company he was building. He knew Donnie was
watching, too. The boy had shown his developing business
sense in the way he'd saved his money and negotiated the

price of his new bicycle. Gordon was pleased with the lifestyle he was establishing for himself and the example he was setting for Donnie. But despite Genesee's increasing success, running it was not without worry. During the summer months, the company always went into the red, meaning they spent more money than they made and still had to pay employees and maintain trucks. This was normal for a heating business, since no one needs fuel for their furnace in the warm months. For that reason, the longevity of the company depended on profits earned in the fall, winter, and early spring.

Most years, people started thinking about buying fuel for heat after Labor Day, when the kids were back in school, but most didn't actually schedule a delivery until they really needed to start heating. Some years, the orders took longer to roll in than others. Gordon and Russ had learned that in a business dependent on weather, you can never get too comfortable. But even understanding that, the summer of 1949 dragged on uncomfortably long. Gordon, a God-fearing, faithful man, prayed for cold weather. But when a record-setting high of seventy-four degrees hit one day in November, he prayed more fervently and tightened his belt.

One would think a warm fall would foreshadow a warm winter, but it doesn't always—especially in Seattle, where the only thing predictable about the weather is its unpredictability. But nonetheless, Gordon and Russ worried. They waited, both patiently and impatiently, for the cold as Thanksgiving, then Christmas, delivered mild temperatures. Then finally, as the New Year was being rung in, Gordon and Russ received sweet relief. On January 1, 1950, an arctic blast hit Seattle, ushering in a record-setting twenty inches of snow, the most in one storm Seattle had ever seen.

That massive snowstorm brought the city to a standstill. It also provided Gordon and Russ with a few new problems to solve. Seattle streets are hilly, and the city wasn't used to getting that much snow. The brothers' concern over a possible warm winter was replaced by the stress of making sure their trucks could get to their customers.

But while the blanket of snow hindered auto traffic, the streets filled with laughing, playing children. Each morning, soon after the newspaper landed on his front porch, Donnie held his breath while he checked the school closure announcements, hoping his school would once again be canceled. Winters with enough snow for sledding were rare, so Donnie took full advantage of the novelty. Parents stationed themselves at intersections to ensure no cars were coming, allowing the kids freedom to fly.

That winter's temperatures stayed low through March, which was good news for the company. But when spring finally arrived, it was greeted like a long-lost friend. Gordon was finally able to slow down,. Once he did, he realized how much stress he'd been under—both with work and at home. Katie was becoming increasingly paralyzed with depression. She was now having a hard time completing daily chores, such as basic cooking and cleaning. Gordon had been trying his best to help out, but he was just so tired.

When tired became exhausted and was then accompanied

by nausea and trouble breathing, Gordon decided it must be more than a result of stress or worry and finally went to the doctor. As it turned out, he was right. He'd been experiencing a series of mild heart attacks. After a trip to the hospital for tests, he was laid up in bed for months.

During this time, Gordon realized he needed to get help for Katie. Cooking had never been something she enjoyed, but she did it because it was her duty. Now Gordon thought hiring someone to help around the house might lift Katie's spirits and boost her energy. He hoped so, since it was getting hard to shield Donnie from Katie's depression. Gordon didn't want to squash the boy's happiness by exposing him unnecessarily to his mother's pain.

As Gordon looked to the future, so did Donnie—who now preferred to be called Don, since he would be starting at Franklin High School in the fall. In typical fourteen-year-old fashion, his interest had started to shift from bikes and baseball to cars and jobs—or to any way he could make money—since he had learned that his own money could buy him his own toys. Now that Don had his Schwinn, he saw it as a means to get from one place to another until he was old enough to drive a car. He began noting the number of high school drivers on the road revving their engines at stop signs, windows rolled down, arms resting casually on the open frame. Sometimes he saw carloads of boys or girls, and other times it was just a boy with a girl riding along. He was intrigued.

Not far from his house, he admired a neighbor's 1940 Ford coupe, parked in the driveway. Sometimes when he'd pedal by on his bicycle, he'd see the backside of a guy bent over the engine of the car—hood up, doors open, various tools lying around, and usually a bottle of Coke nearby. Although Don wasn't particularly interested in learning about mechanics, he really wanted a closer look at that Ford, with its distinguished high flat-topped hood, bumper guards, fender skirts, and white sidewall tires. Despite hardly knowing this older kid, Don offered to help. With limited ability in mechanics, however, he was more like an assistant to a surgeon—just handing over the wrench or holding the greased rag.

From that point on, Don decided it was time to start planning for his next big purchase—a car. Don's passion for cars grew daily, and he loved talking to his dad about the latest models and features, as well as the classics. He also started to devise a plan in his head and setting goals, a characteristic he'd inherited from his dad.

By junior year in high school, Don was working at the Serve-U Grocery in Hillman City, earning $1.13 per hour. The manager, impressed by Don's good marks in school, allowed him to work the 5:00–11:00 p.m. shift—an option not given to every student employee. It was a real job with real responsibility. Interacting with adults was easy for Don. He was developing his customer-service skills and impressed his boss with his good work ethic. Most of all, he enjoyed the independence.

Don was still saving his money, his eagerness to buy his own car reinforced by his interest in a new girl he'd begun to notice in Mr. Caddey's biology class at Franklin High School. Anita Salmela was new to the school. She had just moved to the neighborhood from the Kitsap Peninsula. With her blue eyes, blonde hair, and petite figure, Don was sure he wasn't the only one attracted to her.

She was quiet, though; not shy, but an observer. She made eye contact and smiled. She appeared to be listening to the teacher and took notes like a good student should. She sat at her desk confidently. She didn't fidget with her hair or bite her pencil. She just looked like a nice girl, and Don wanted to get to know her. But when he tried to make conversation, he was at an unusual loss for words. Normally Don could strike up a conversation with a lamppost. But with Anita, the only words he managed to utter during his first few attempts at conversation were questions he already knew the answers to, though he asked anyway. "What's the assignment, again?" She politely told him, then continued packing up her things as students funneled into the halls.

A few weeks later on a Sunday morning, Don sat in the back seat of his dad's car, his mom in the passenger seat, as they drove north on Rainier Avenue on their way to Whitman Avenue Gospel Chapel, previously Hope Gospel Hall. They were listening to a broadcast from downtown Seattle at the Union Gospel Mission, a ministry that had started as a soup kitchen during the Great Depression and continued sheltering and ministering to the homeless. Don's ears perked up when he heard the legendary *Seattle Times* sportswriter Royal Brougham announce, "Our next hymn will be led by two Franklin High School students. But first, a word from our sponsor." Don knew quite a few kids at the high school, but he didn't know who would be singing on the radio.

"Dad, can ya turn up the radio? I wonder who from Franklin is gonna sing."

Gordon turned up the volume. He would have turned down the volume for the duration if the sponsor message had been about cigarettes or alcohol. Katie didn't like hearing a sales pitch for products she considered sinful. But this time it was an ad for Frederick & Nelson, the popular department store in downtown Seattle and birthplace of the Frango chocolate mint—one of Katie's favorites.

Royal Brougham's voice returned. "And now we'll hear from the Salmela sisters. They'll lead us in singing 'Great Is Thy Faithfulness.'"

Don's right foot hit the floor after flying off his left knee, where it had been sitting casually just a moment before. He grabbed the back of the front seat bench and scooted himself forward, getting as close to the radio as he could without climbing over into the front seat between his parents. "Oh gee, I know them! Anita is in my biology class!" Don stared intently at the vertical white line on the radio panel, as if fixing his eyes on the dial would guarantee that the sound transmitted without static. He didn't tell his parents he was sweet on Anita right then. That would have interrupted his ability to listen closely.

The sisters sang, and Don listened. "All I have needed Thy hand hath provided; / Great is Thy faithfulness, Lord, unto me." As if Don hadn't been enamored enough, he was now a puppy getting a belly rub. Anita's voice was a roadblock to all other senses. He didn't see or hear anything else on that ride to church—just her. And, "Great is Thy Faithfulness" had just become his favorite hymn.

Now Don was more determined than ever to buy his own car. The rising popularity of cars had changed the dating game in the 1950s. Now that teenagers were making their own money and could buy their own cars, they were able to go out on dates, away from their parents. Sometimes they just cruised through town, showing off their cars, or their dates, or both. They could be seen in masses at drive-in diners and drive-in movie theaters. Teenagers in the '50s were experiencing such a different lifestyle than their parents had, it was like they had formed a culture of their own.

Don had his eye on a '49 Ford coupe. He hoped that once he had it, he could take Anita out on a date. At school, he talked all year about how he was working and saving his money to buy that car. He planned on having enough to buy it over the summer. In fact, he talked about it so much, almost every signature in his yearbook that spring read something like, "Dear Don, you're a swell guy, good luck getting your car this summer."

Just a few days into his senior year, while walking down the stairs at Franklin, Don felt a tap on his shoulder. "Did you get your car?" It was Anita. She stood on the step above him, so they were eye to eye. She had startled him, but in the best way. She smiled while waiting for his answer.

"Well, yeah, I got it. You want a ride?" Then, before she could even answer, he followed with, "I'll give you a ride."

It wasn't the '49 Ford coupe he'd originally wanted. But once he had all his money, he found a powder-blue '49 Chevy convertible for $1,100. It was almost perfect. He'd really wanted white sidewall tires, but the Chevy didn't come with those. Having just enough to cover the expense of the car, he couldn't afford new tires.

Both Don and Gordon agreed that tires were as important to the look of a car as shoes were to a businessman in a suit. But this detail was often overlooked by anyone not enthusiastic about cars. Katie was one of those people. To her, cars served the purpose of getting you from place to place. Aesthetic upgrades were not necessary or worth spending money on.

Since Gordon was sympathetic to Don's fancy for whitewall tires, he wanted to buy them for him. But first they needed to justify the expense to Katie. She often told Gordon he was "spoiling" Don—that their son didn't need such frivolous things. She would definitely consider buying Don new tires just to complete the look of his car an act of spoiling. But if it were about safety, that was another thing. So Don and Gordon took that approach. They showed Katie the car and pointed out the wear and tear on the original tires. Just like that, she said, "Well, we ought to get him some new tires, don't you think, Gordon?"

Don couldn't have been more proud of his new powder-blue convertible Chevy. It was his baby. If he wasn't driving it or showing it off to friends and neighbors, he was washing it. He washed and polished it every day. He made sure those whitewalls stayed white, although eventually, his diligence worked against him. He scrubbed the whites of the tires so frequently, within the year he went right through the white rubber, exposing the black underneath.

On the day Don was to give Anita a ride in his new car, students flooded out the doors of Franklin High School after the final bell. It was a sunny day in September, so the top would be down. Don led Anita to where he had parked his new car behind the high school. She said all the right things to please Don about his purchase: "A convertible, wow!" and "Oh, it looks swell," and "Such a nice color."

She sat at the far right side of the bench and held her scarf snug over her head in an attempt to keep her hair in place against the wind. Don waved as he passed people he knew, sometimes tapping the horn or flashing his lights. He wanted to be sure he was seen on this particular drive down Rainier Avenue.

The only problem with this scenario was that Anita already had a boyfriend: a military guy a few years older, serving in California. This was common information, and Don already knew it. He understood this wasn't a date. It was just a friendly show of his new car, although he wished it could have been more.

When Don got home from school that day, he sat heavily on a chair at the kitchen table. His mother noticed his somber mood, and asked, "Well, what's the matter with you?" Katie didn't sugar coat anything. She was direct and to the point. With strangers, she was always polite, but not overly so. She wouldn't ask how one was feeling if she didn't genuinely want to know.

Don told his mother about Anita and how he'd met her in biology class. He told her how pretty she was and about her smile. He told her that even when she wasn't smiling, she smiled with her big blue eyes. He told her that while she was sort of quiet—at least relative to some of the girls he knew— she had a beautiful voice. He reminded his mother that she was the girl they'd heard on the radio that day. "Remember?" he said. He knew these details would be important to his mother.

"Well, then what's the matter?" Katie asked.

"Well," Don explained. "she already has a boyfriend." Don's hands went up and landed heavily on the kitchen table. He shook his head in surrender.

"Well," Katie said matter-of-factly. "The best man wins."

With that simple yet practical advice from his mother, Don gained a little more courage. With it, he was able to make light conversation when he passed Anita in the halls. Soon, he learned she had a job at Gai's Northwest Bakery in the Central

District and that she rode the bus to work. It did not take Don much detective work to find out exactly where Anita caught the bus. Then, coincidentally (or not) Don just happened to drive by the corner of Graham Street and Rainier Avenue exactly when Anita stood waiting. Of course, he offered her a ride, and she accepted.

Pretty soon, it appeared as though Don was winning the *better man* race. Just a few Chevy convertible rides later, Anita broke it off with the California boyfriend and started dating Don. By the end of their senior year, Don and Anita were going steady and had been voted "steadiest couple" by their class, as printed in their high school yearbook.

As the school year wrapped up, it was an exciting, culminating time full of celebrations. Don felt pretty good about how high school had gone. After graduation, some of his classmates planned to find full-time jobs that suited them, while others would just increase their hours at their current jobs. Some graduates would enlist in the military, and a few— less than 30 percent—would enroll in college.

It was somewhat expected, both culturally and by his family, that Don would go to work for Genesee after high school. But that idea didn't appeal to Don. He knew Genesee was an option, but he wasn't sure he wanted to settle down in the company where he'd spent his childhood. Now, getting ready to graduate from high school, he didn't really feel like an adult. He definitely didn't feel ready yet for an adultlike full-time job.

Don had received good grades in school, and he liked being a student. Since he didn't know what he wanted to do for a career, continuing on to the University of Washington sounded like as good a plan as any. Even better, Anita was planning on attending the university as well.

In June of 1954, both Don and Anita graduated from Franklin High School. The first of his family to wear a cap and gown, Don felt elated. The only thing that bothered him was the fact that his mother was not in attendance. Sadly, Katie's depression had become severe—so bad this time that she couldn't leave the house. Though she still had phases of being better or worse, over time her situation had deteriorated. No one knew what to do about it.

In the Seattle Civic Auditorium, Don sat in his cap and gown among his peers arranged in straight lines facing the stage. He looked around at the faces—in the rows next to, in front of, and behind him. They had all been on this high school journey together, some since their first years in school. Now, like a firework propelled into the air, then exploding into stars of light in all directions, they, too, would go separate ways. Sitting there, Don felt really good about his decision to go to college.

Meanwhile, from the audience, Gordon watched his son. The green-and-black tassel that hung from Donnie's cap danced as he smiled and shook hands with every teacher, each one giving him an approving nod. Gordon had never been to a graduation, and this was exciting. He thought about Si, the importance that family had held for his father, and then himself. He believed in Donnie's loyalty, his concern for both his mother's and father's health, and, perhaps, for the family business. He also understood his son's desire for independence and his longing for the opportunity to make his own way, and he accepted it.

The kid wanted to go to college. How could he argue with that?

CHAPTER TEN

1954–1958

The future belongs to those who believe
in the beauty of their dreams.
—ELEANOR ROOSEVELT

WHEN THE STUDENTS ARRIVED ON THE UNIVERSITY OF Washington campus in late September 1954, it looked like fall but felt like summer. Leaves on the cherry trees lining the perimeter of the quad had just started to turn from vibrant green to varying shades of brown, yellow, and orange. Students wore short sleeves instead of cardigan sweaters and walked with purpose, books in arms, on the red brick paths that crisscrossed the quad in a triangular pattern. Don knew almost immediately that he would like the university. It was full of smart, interesting, engaging people.

He registered for classes that would lead to a bachelor's degree in business, with no specific idea of what he would actually do with that diploma. But he didn't waste a second thinking about it. This was exactly where Don wanted to be.

Still going steady, Don and Anita commuted to and from

campus together every day. Don picked her up in his powder-blue Chevy. He kept the top up for their daily drives to school so as not to mess Anita's hair before classes. But on nice days in the afternoons, Don loved nothing more than driving down Rainier Avenue with Anita in his car and the top down. She scooched right up next to him, as close as she could on the white bench seat. Don's left wrist rested on top of the steering wheel and his right arm stretched out on the seat behind her.

At first, Anita wanted to study accounting. She was good at math and thought she would enjoy analyzing and balancing financial records for a small business someday. But counselors at the university discouraged her from that choice. Because she was a woman, they thought she would likely only end up working as a bookkeeper, not an actual accountant. Teaching and nursing were the two areas of study they recommended for her.

That infuriated Anita, as she told Don on their ride home. She felt she was easily just as smart as, if not smarter than, any of the men taking those accounting classes.

"It just makes me so mad." Anita's brows furrowed. She looked at Don, waiting for him to say something that would help.

"Well, teaching's all right." Don shrugged. Anita turned her head to look out the side window. "Well, isn't it?" Don thought she would make a good teacher, and that it was a respectable profession.

"Well, I guess so." Anita sulked, still visibly mad.

Don didn't know what else to say. He didn't understand why she would be so mad about that suggestion, when she'd originally wanted to attend the teacher's college at Seattle Pacific but couldn't because it was too expensive. Tuition at the University of Washington cost $175 per year, an amount her family could afford. It wasn't until Anita started attending the university that she had even gotten the idea to be an accountant.

Don wasn't sure if she was mad at him, mad at the counselor, or just mad that someone had told her she couldn't be or do something. She didn't say another word the whole ride home. She wouldn't look at him either. She just looked out the window and sat on the far end of the bench seat like she had when they first started dating. By the time he dropped her off at her house, she told him she wasn't in the mood to go on their usual Friday night date. She shut the door and headed into her house.

Don drove away shaking his head, still not exactly sure what he'd done wrong. Anita's independence and intelligence were characteristics he was attracted to, but so was her calm, soft-spoken demeanor. His Aunt Beulah was a bookkeeper, and to Don, that career suited her. While Beulah was generous, spoiling her only nephew with nice gifts such as the fine wristwatch she'd given him for graduation, she was also a little cynical and gruff—not like Anita at all. He thought Anita would make a better teacher than accountant. She was warm, nurturing, and liked working with people. Maybe he should have told her that. In the end, Anita simply accepted her circumstance and made the most of it. She, like Don, was a rule-follower. She completed assignments, reported to work on time, and took advice that was given to her.

By the following Friday, Anita was back next to Don in the front seat, telling him about her education classes as they drove to one of their favorite date-night spots. Burgermaster in the University District was the place to be. It was where college students buzzed in their tailfin Chevys and whitewall-tired Studebakers. The waitresses wore roller-skates to take orders and deliver food. Don wasn't sure if life could get any better than this. He put his arm around Anita and waited for his burger and shake.

Don wasn't the only one living the high life in 1955. Gordon and Russ were making more than a decent living. Heating oil had become the preferred and sought-after fuel for homes in Seattle. Although there were several other local heating oil companies that would always be their competition, many of Genesee's customers claimed they could never buy fuel from anyone else. It had been during Seattle's lowest of low points—the Great Depression—when people were barely able to put food on their tables, that Genesee Fuel had given them heat, forgiving their debts and chalking it up to just being a good neighbor.

The only other form of heat available, and used by very few, was manufactured gas. The Seattle Gas Light Company originally manufactured this type of gas on the north shore of Lake Union at a location called Brown's Point, later known as Gasworks Park. Seattle's gas streetlamps had burned this manmade gas as far back as the late 1800s, as did a few private homes that could afford that luxury at the time. The gas was originally manufactured from coal, then later petroleum oil. But its popularity peaked in about 1930. By 1955, it wasn't even the slightest threat to the heating oil business. The gas plant had become quite controversial and unpopular, as it was a source of major water, soil, and visible air pollution, particularly in the neighborhood of Wallingford.

Gordon thought back to the decision to take on oil ten years prior. Had they not taken that risk, the company wouldn't have survived. Coal had been quickly dying as a source of residential heat, and by 1955, the only reason Genesee Fuel kept its few remaining coal customers was out of loyalty. His and Russ's only regret about taking on heating oil was that they hadn't done it sooner. But now they had a fine company and did well for themselves. Gordon felt good about where things were headed. He was building a legacy. *By the time Donnie gets his college degree,* he thought, *why wouldn't he want to be a part of this?*

Since now they had money to spend, instead of buying used when they purchased cars, both Gordon and Russ bought brand-new ones. As always, Gordon had to buy the best. A 1955 Cadillac Coupe de Ville cost about $6,000, almost double an average person's yearly income at the time. Katie shook her head at the expense, although she did enjoy the ride.

Even though the business was doing well, Gordon and Russ knew they couldn't get too comfortable. They'd been raised on this understanding, starting back on the farm in Leduc: conditions are unpredictable. Another financial disaster, a new natural disaster, or just a string of extremely warm winters could bring the company to a halt. Other than the cars, they knew not to live extravagantly, because in any given year, anything could happen.

Soon, something did. This event, unlike the stock market crash or the onset of World War II, hardly made the news. But for Gordon and Russ, it posed the biggest threat of all.

In 1956, natural gas arrived to the area from Canada via the Northwest Pipeline. Production of manufactured gas on Brown's Point ceased, and the Seattle Gas Company turned into a larger entity, the Washington Natural Gas Company, which would later be acquired by Puget Sound Energy. Gordon and Russ knew this would affect their business. They just didn't know exactly how soon or to what extent. They also didn't know what they could do about it. The last time a new fuel had arrived in town, they'd simply added that fuel to their inventory. But natural gas was a utility, like electricity or water, supplied through pipelines regulated by the government. The company could not simply switch fuels as it had done before.

At this point, all the brothers could do was wait and see. They had been in this situation many times before. It was not a feeling they wanted to be comfortable with, but not knowing if they would be in business within the next year was a reality of their industry. This time, the threat that lurked around the corner felt bigger. They didn't have access to this new fuel. Natural gas was generating buzz; it was said to be cleaner and more efficient than heating oil. Russ and Gordon feared that if it were here to stay, it would mean their demise.

Sure enough, over the next few years, natural gas did become a drain on their business. But fortunately, it was more of a smoldering stick than a raging flame. The transition from heating oil to natural gas was a little more complicated than the conversion from a coal-burning furnace to an oil-burning one. For a customer to switch from oil to gas, they had to pay for the underground pipe from the roadway into their house, which was an expense not everyone could afford. This made for a slower loss of business. Customers had to have a chunk of money to make the switch; therefore, turnover happened at a modest rate.

Still, the general feeling at Genesee Fuel was, as Russ would say: "We're done. Finished. This will be the end of us." Natural gas was the new kid in town. It was fresher, cleaner, cheaper, and the new modern thing. It was hard to compete with that. The population in the area was still growing, and newly built houses now sported brand-new natural gas furnaces instead of oil furnaces. So, like the orchestra playing on the deck of the sinking *Titanic*, Genesee Fuel continued in business as it plateaued and started its gradual decline.

Still, while Genesee Fuel may have been a small, independently owned fuel company, it would not go down without a fight. By the spring of 1958, Russ and Gordon knew they needed a new strategy. The only problem was that once again, the brothers were at odds as to the company's direction. Russ wanted to accept defeat but ride it out until his retirement. He had less generational skin in the game. He'd made a good career out of Genesee, but had neither the energy nor a good reason to put up a fight. Gordon held the opposite opinion. He wasn't ready to retire. He had Don, who was set to graduate in June. He wanted the business he'd built to be a viable option for him—if he wanted it.

Meanwhile, winter quarter of his senior year of college was wrapping up, and Don felt no closer to knowing what he would do after graduation than he had when he'd started as a freshman. He thought about going to law school, or business school. He wished his dad would give him some guidance, some encouragement, anything. But he didn't.

The only thing Don knew for certain was that after graduation, he wanted to marry Anita. It had been four years since he'd felt a tap on his shoulder on those steps at Franklin High and she agreed to go for a ride in his car. He could still feel the butterflies that had fluttered in his stomach as they walked to his parking spot on Mount Baker Boulevard that day. They had encountered a few bumps in the road, but now he knew: he loved everything about her. She had faith, had been raised in a Christian home, was independent yet easygoing, loved her family, treated people with respect, and valued education.

Both were set to graduate in June. Don had picked out an engagement ring around Thanksgiving and had been making payments toward it with every paycheck. With spring on the horizon, he picked a date and the restaurant where he would propose. Just as he was fond of cars, Don had an appetite for fine dining. He either loved a good burger and a thick milkshake, or a tender steak and crème brûlée. Anything in between, he could live without. As often as he could afford, he took Anita up to Queen Anne Hill with its view of Lake Union. They dined at Canlis, where waitresses gracefully paced in kimonos, or they went to the Cloud Room, the penthouse space on top of the Camlin Hotel that frequently hosted famous faces such as Frank Sinatra, Dean Martin, and Miles Davis.

For this occasion, he picked Moultry's Four Seas restaurant, the old ship turned into a restaurant with a pirate theme, on Lake Union. Anita bought a new dress in anticipation of this date. She often took the opportunity to buy a new outfit when Don announced he would be taking her out to a fancy restaurant.

In keeping with his family and traditional values, Don had already asked Anita's father, Jack Salmela, for her hand. Jack was born in Winlock, Washington, to immigrants from Finland. He had only learned to speak English when he started school at age six. He had a classic stoic Scandinavian nature but a kind, generous heart, and he was constantly offering to help anyone in need. Although he didn't show much emotion, he made it known that he couldn't have been happier for his oldest daughter to marry Don. Both Anita's parents, as well as her older brother, Nik, and her younger sister, Mary Lou, thought the world of Don.

Once the decision was made and the ring purchased, it took every ounce of Don's being to wait for the moment he envisioned. Patience didn't come naturally for Don. Within minutes of sitting down across the table from Anita, Don pulled out the little black velvet box, opened it up, and plunked it down in front of Anita.

"Well, what do you think?" Although Don could make conversation with anyone, he had a harder time putting his deepest sentiments into words.

Her eyes lit up, and she smiled and looked at Don. He knew she was waiting for more from him, but he also knew she knew his heart and his intentions. After a long pause, Don said, plain and simple, "Well, do you want to get married?"

Anita had always had a hard time fighting tears. Happy or sad, they welled up within seconds of either emotion. "Well, yes, I do." She pursed her lips, trying not to get so caught up in emotions that the tears would spill over. Once that happened, it was hard to stop them.

Don took the ring out of the box and reached for her hand. Anita helped it onto her finger, and gazed at the emerald-cut diamond with two baguettes on either side, set in white gold. It was simple yet sweet, and perfectly suited to her —both the ring, and the proposal.

Over a dinner they hardly tasted in their excitement, Anita looked at her ring often. She could hardly wait to show her family. When Don brought her home that night, they were all there, including her brother, Nik, and his wife, Beverly, who just happened to be in town visiting her parents. Upon seeing her whole family, Anita hardly got the words out before the joyful tears started flowing. Anita looked down at her ring, and just as she moved her hand to show it to her brother, a teardrop rolled down her face and onto her shiny new jewels.

"Aw, it's all right, Nita," said Nik. "It won't melt. *A diamond is forever.*" Nik was always able to lighten the mood with a simple, quiet one-liner, and the popular De Beers advertising slogan had been on the tip of everyone's tongue in those days.

Graduation day was June 11, 1958. It was a gorgeous, clear-blue-sky day in Seattle. Don sat in his graduation cap and gown in the Hec Edmundson Pavilion, the fieldhouse named after a longtime University of Washington Huskies track and basketball coach. As he sat there, he thought about his future. He turned around to look for Anita but couldn't find her in the sea of graduates. She would have been at the back of the alphabetically ordered crowd. Don didn't pay much attention to the details of the commencement speaker's speech. He was thinking about his accomplishment, and still pondering registering for law school.

Outside the stadium, he found his mother and dad. This time, Katie had been there to witness his graduation. She had been receiving electroconvulsive therapy, also known as shock treatment, for her severe depression. She smiled, hugged Don, and told him how proud of him she was. Don hadn't realized how severely depressed she had been until he saw her well again.

Walking along Montlake Boulevard toward their car, a big black Lincoln pulled up and the back window rolled down. Washington State Governor Al Rosellini leaned out. "Hello, Gordon. Congratulations to your boy."

One of several graduation speakers that day, Al Rosellini had grown up in the Rainier Valley and was a friend of Gordon's. "Thank you, my friend." Gordon reached over and shook the governor's hand.

Don straightened his stance and quickly offered his handshake. "Thank you, sir." He noted that everywhere he went, his dad seemed to know someone. People respected him as a businessman. Who would have thought he'd once been a farmer?

Don had been struggling with his next move for months now. He had thoroughly enjoyed his time as a student at Washington, and he wasn't ready for it all to be over. He knew UW had a good law school, or maybe he could continue his education by getting a master's in business administration somewhere else, like Stanford or Harvard. He knew he could do that. He had the drive and the means, yet lacked courage. If only someone were to say, "Don, you'd make a good lawyer. Why don't you go to law school?" he would do it, without hesitation. But neither his dad, or his uncle, or his mother would ever say that. In their eyes, he had enough education, and it was time to appreciate that and get to work. Don understood their point of view. His parents were of a different generation, culture, and socioeconomic background. But Don wasn't sure he was ready to settle.

At his graduation celebration meal that gorgeous day in Seattle, Don looked at the people surrounding him—his parents, Anita, and her parents. So much love and support were right here in his hometown of Seattle. In that moment, he was far too happy to make any life-changing decisions.

Meanwhile, conversations between Gordon and Russ were now all about what to do about natural gas. Its presence was a problem they hadn't found a way to solve. They bounced back and forth between "We'll be all right for a while" and "We're doomed." But it was mostly the latter. Don had been listening to this cyclical talk for a couple years. Now equipped with a shiny degree, he piped in.

"Well, sounds like you need a salesman."

CHAPTER ELEVEN

1958–1962

The three great essentials to achieve anything worthwhile are, first, hard work; second, stick-to-itiveness; third, common sense.
—THOMAS EDISON

THE DAY AFTER GRADUATION, DON PUT ON HIS SUIT, TIED HIS necktie, and looked at himself in the mirror. He stood tall and confident and felt as good as he looked. He was a college graduate, ready to go out into the world and make his mark. But, for the summer, he would work as a salesman at Genesee Fuel. Law school or getting an MBA could wait.

Entering through the back door to announce his arrival on his first day, he ran right into Russ. "Oh, hello, Uncle Russ." Don grabbed his necktie and ran his hand down the length of it, feeling the fabric against his chest. "I'm ready. Where should I start?"

Russ stood there and looked him up and down. Although he'd never said so out loud, Russ had given Don the impression that he didn't think much of his college education. He'd made it clear that he and Gordon had built the company with hard work and determination. They hadn't needed that expensive piece of paper.

Russ nodded, then handed Don a broom. "Start here."

Surprised, and a bit deflated, Don took the broom. "Well, Uncle Russ, I just graduated from the University of Washington with a bachelor's degree in business administration."

Russ didn't skip a beat. "Well then, let me show you how to use that."

To Don, sweeping the floor didn't feel like a job for a salesman, let alone a college graduate. He did, in time, understand what his uncle was getting at. In a small business, people had to be willing to do all the jobs, regardless of what title any piece of paper gave them. Don knew, too, that he had been "the kid" for years. He would have to earn his place within the company and prove his value.

Although Gordon and Russ historically hadn't needed to go out and win customers, times had changed. A good reputation wasn't enough anymore. Natural gas was picking off customers, giving their previous providers no chance to get them back. Once a customer converted their oil furnace to gas, their oil tank was decommissioned, and that was the end of it. Other oil companies were feeling the pinch, too, and were now going door to door, trying to convince Genesee Fuel's customers to switch to them. Sometimes, they succeeded.

Don had finally convinced Gordon and Russ that in order to keep their business, they needed to fight back. It was time to get more aggressive. It was time to convince homeowners who still had oil furnaces that Genesee Fuel was the best heating oil company in Seattle—and no one had more of a vested interest in getting that job done than Don. He had the confidence, the pride, the determination, the drive, the ideas—and the diploma—making him the natural choice. He knew he had to make it work—not just to prove it to his uncle, but to prove it to himself. He also knew how much the company meant to his dad.

During college, Don continued working at the Serve-U Grocery but at the Montlake location instead of Hillman City. Part of his responsibilities there had been delivering groceries. But, he didn't just drop bags of meat and potatoes on a customer's doorstep; he visited with his regular customers and got to know them. Now, on his first day on the job as salesman, Don went back to each of those homeowners. He talked to them about his recent graduation and his new summer job. By the end of the day, he walked back into the Genesee Fuel office holding his head high. He couldn't wait to tell Russ. He'd brought in eight new accounts on day one. Russ nearly fell out of his chair.

While Don spent his first post-graduation days knocking on doors, Anita spent hers with her sister Mary Lou, shopping for churches, dresses, and cakes. When Anita found her favorite dress, she had Mary Lou sketch it, and then asked a friend of the family, a seamstress, to make it for her. When Phil Gai of Gai's Bakery, Anita's former boss, learned about Anita's upcoming wedding, he thoughtfully offered to make her wedding cake as his gift to Don and Anita. He must have thought very highly of Anita, since he provided a 500-serving cake for a 250-guest wedding.

In the midst of the wedding planning, Anita was also interviewing for teaching jobs in various school districts. In the end, she was given multiple offers, but settled on a fifth-grade position at a brand-new school in South Central School District. She was set to start in late August, just after her honeymoon.

On August 8, 1958, Don and Anita were married. As a wedding/graduation gift, Gordon and Katie gave them a brand-new 1958 Chevy Impala, black with a white top. Though it was customary at the time for the groomsman and bridesmaids to decorate the wedding getaway car with various ribbons and cans tied to the back, Don dreaded this tradition. He could hardly stand having a speck of dirt on his old car, let alone his brand-new one. Don needed to come up with a plan to foil the shenanigans, and he knew the perfect person. Don's best man and the future husband of Anita's sister, Bob Joss, was always up for a good scheme.

"Bob, I don't want the guys messing up my new car with 'just married' and all that stuff."

Bob smiled and laughed, knowing how Don felt about his cars. "Oh yeah? So what are you going to do, hide it?"

"Well, yeah. I was thinking we could use your car as a decoy."

"Sure, I don't mind. In fact, I'll even be your chauffeur!"

So, with the help of a few allies, Don and Bob came up with an elaborate plan. An employee at Genesee lived in Wallingford, a neighborhood close to the University Congregational Church, where the wedding would take place. He agreed to hide Don's new car, the real getaway car, in his garage.

The plan worked. Promptly after the reception downstairs in the church, Anita changed into her going-away outfit: a chocolate-brown dress with a matching jacket, a cream-colored cloche, and matching wrist-length gloves. As Mr. and Mrs., the newlyweds climbed into a car and peered through a back window spray-painted with the words "Just Married." They waved goodbye to their guests, cans on strings rattling and ribbons blowing off the back of Bob's car. Just a couple miles down the road they switched it out for their new clean Chevy, then headed south on their honeymoon: a two-week road trip to Disneyland and Las Vegas via the Oregon Coast.

Back at work, Don's summer of sales had proven successful. By late fall of that year, in order to keep up with the business he'd brought in, they needed him driving an oil truck instead. It had been such a busy summer, Don hadn't had time to think about his next move. But knowing he had brought in the new accounts, he was happy to accommodate. He fondly remembered his ride-alongs as a kid with Ed. This time, he would get to be the one behind the wheel of the big rig.

As it turned out, he enjoyed the change of pace and the challenges the new role brought. He and longtime driver Frank Richmond quickly developed a friendly competition over how many gallons they could deliver in a day. Frank teased him that Don got all the big tanks, or "good accounts," since he was the son of the boss. Don countered that Frank had the newer truck and nicer equipment. Don liked the challenge of making his deliveries more efficient, but he also found humor in the competition. More than that, he simply enjoyed driving a truck, pulling the hose, satisfying customers with a full tank, and working for a company he felt was in some ways part of his soul.

As another summer approached, it was time for the company to upgrade some of its equipment. Since the company had added heating oil ten years prior, the two old oil trucks had covered hundreds of thousands of miles and delivered hundreds of thousands of gallons of oil. It was time for new ones. Don enjoyed traveling as much as he liked driving trucks, so he offered to pick up the new trucks from the manufacturer in Pontiac, Michigan, and drive them back, one piggybacking on the other. Since Anita would be on summer break from her teaching job, Don thought it would be a perfect opportunity for her to ride along.

Anita might have had other ideas of ways to spend her summer vacation, but of course she agreed. In the spring before they left, she told Don it had become quite a joke amongst her teacher friends. When those friends headed to the beach, or the mountains, or wherever they were headed, Anita and Don flew to the Midwest.

Although it probably wasn't the most glamorous summer, it did prove to be a bit of an adventure. On a hot Sunday afternoon in Minnesota during the return trip, a state trooper pulled Don and Anita over just as they crossed the state border from Wisconsin. He glanced at Anita and spoke to Don.

"Can't drive your truck through here on Sundays."

"Well, officer, I just picked up these new trucks and I need to get them back to Seattle."

"Not today. There's a sign right there, 'No trucks on Sunday.' You'll need to pull off at that next exit. If you don't, I'll write you a ticket."

It was clear there was no negotiating with this officer on the blue laws that considered driving a truck "work," which was not to be done on the day of rest.

Off the highway at the nearest gas station, Anita sat on her suitcase in the shade of the truck while Don made a phone call to his cousin, Don McLellan. Since Don had grown up an only child, keeping up relationships with his cousins was important to him. He, like his dad, had a herdsman mentality. Regardless of geography, he kept tabs on everyone. Just a few hours later, Don and Anita were picked up and taken to cousin Don's house in Minneapolis to stay the night.

Back on the road the next day, they had a good laugh about their time in Minnesota. But there were also long stretches when they were quiet, just thinking introspectively. Don reflected on his summer job that had turned into a year-long one. He realized he liked the work better than he had thought he would, and he was feeling pretty vital to the company now. But like his dad and uncle, he was worried about how the company's future stacked up against natural gas.

Once they crossed into Washington State, still on Interstate 90, the landscape became more familiar. The evergreen trees and the Cascade Mountains felt like home, and naturally their conversations started circling their lives—both current and future—in Seattle. They both wanted children eventually, but didn't want to rush into it. Anita loved her job as a teacher and was adored by her students. But the possibility of law school or business school was still in Don's head and causing an internal tug of war. *Do I still want that?* he wondered.

It seemed to Don that as he and Anita drove closer to home, law school and business school got even further away. Fortunately though, the road he was traveling was comfortable, and for the time being, it seemed like the right one to be on, despite the uncertainty that loomed.

By 1961, natural gas was more than a hazard Don's family business faced. It was a major threat. The Washington Natural Gas Company's advertising campaign was making an impression on people, with its the iconic little blue flame and a promise to take the customer into the modern age of fuel. The company had also started taking an aggressive approach to acquiring accounts from heating oil users, as they offered to lease gas conversion kits to heating oil customers for $1.95 per month. This meant that customers didn't have to have a chunk of money up front to make the switch. Natural gas was also quite a bit cheaper per unit of heat than oil, so turnovers were picking up pace. Genesee was feeling the squeeze.

"Heating oil is safer and gives warmer heat," Don told homeowners, who often had children running around. "Oil is also non-explosive. Natural gas will blow up your whole house if it's even in the vicinity of a flame." He could often talk people out of switching when he explained it this way. Other people disregarded him. Captured by the lure of the blue flame, they just wanted the cheaper, modern fuel.

These homeowners weren't the only ones thrilled by the prospect of modernity. The city of Seattle was getting ready for an event so epic, it would forever change the Seattle skyline. The United States was deep in the Space Race with Russia, and the Seattle-based Boeing company was working on aerospace travel design. So when Seattle won the bid to host the 1962 World's Fair, its space-age theme, called Century 21, couldn't have been more fitting.

In the months before the fair, the Space Needle emerged against the skyline. A modern-day Eiffel Tower with an orange-painted, spaceship-like top, it became an iconic symbol of Seattle and of futuristic times. For dramatic effect, flames periodically shot from the needle that pointed skyward—flames ironically fueled by natural gas. As opening day approached, the monorail, a modern air train, was launched, connecting downtown to the fairgrounds. A "See You in Seattle" campaign summoned the world to come see the city's vision of the future. Then, on April 21, 1962, President Kennedy officially announced the opening of the fair via telephone broadcast.

"I am honored to open the Seattle World's Fair today. What we show is achieved with great effort in the fields of science, technology, and industry. These accomplishments are a bridge which will carry us confidently toward the twenty-first century."

The city was abuzz with excitement for the worldwide attraction right at home. Visitors flew for hours or drove for days to attend the first international fair to be held in the United States in decades. Don and Anita ate Belgian waffles and played the fair games. Don, attracted to the baseball throwing, had to show off his childhood skills to Anita. Remembering "Old Woody" and his days at the Rainier Beach Playfield, Don hit the target, winning a giant stuffed bear. Anita picked the color, yellow, for their soon-to-be son or daughter. At the time of the fair, Anita was six months pregnant.

No one was more thrilled about the impending arrival of a baby than Gordon. He pestered Anita almost daily with "How's that baby doing?" and "When are you going to have that baby?" Don didn't remember his grandfather Si, but he'd heard how excited he was to have a grandson. He'd also heard how hard times were back then—in the midst of the Depression. That era of Seattle was as strange as a foreign country. Gordon talked about waiting for Donnie to arrive and feeling anxious and nervous about everything. Now, he said, he felt only joy in anticipation for the birth of a grandchild.

Finally, on September 4, 1962, Leslie Ann was born. Anita and Don brought her home to an apartment in the Seward Park area, not far from the office. Soon after, they bought a house in the Rainier View neighborhood, a classic one-story house newly built, with a low-pitched roof and an attached carport. One step led to the front door, and there was a splash of red brick under the front window. It had a small front yard and a bigger, fenced-in backyard.

Don was deep in the business now, the idea of law school

finally laid to rest. Although things had fallen comfortably into place, the worrying question of the business's longevity was increasingly taking up space in Don's head. This company had turned his dad and uncle from farmers to businessmen, Canadians to Americans. Don had been born into Genesee Fuel, though, and it had always been a part of him. Finally, Don was beginning to appreciate that he was who he was, and where he was, because of this business.

He wanted to embrace the future, technology, and science of the modern world that President Kennedy had cited. But could their heating oil business survive in the future depicted at the World's Fair? Don wondered and worried. In the business of fuel, heating oil was falling further and further behind in the race for all things modern. Oil was considered old-school, and gas represented the future.

CHAPTER TWELVE

1963–1964

You may encounter many defeats, but you must not be defeated. In fact, it may be necessary to encounter the defeats, so you can know who you are, what you can rise from, how you can still come out of it.

—MAYA ANGELOU

THE SMELL OF A FRESHLY MOWED LAWN AND THE SIGHT OF cherry trees in bloom are welcome signs of spring in Seattle. In the heating business, those indicators also mark the end of the busy season. It was a typical spring day in 1963 when Don walked into the office, but what was not typical was that Russ wouldn't be there.

His retirement had been forthcoming for the last couple years. He was fifty-eight, had no children, and was just tired of entertaining new ideas on how to fight the latest natural gas campaign. He had made plenty of money and decided that Port Angeles, on the Olympic Peninsula, was where he would like to move. He could trade in his classic, turn-of-the-century brick home in Mount Baker for a much bigger piece of land and a nice newer home in Port Angeles.

Beulah, however, wasn't really on board with that idea. She liked city living and all its glamour and convenience. But Russ did as Russ wanted, and Beulah followed. Over forty years before, Russ had run from his rural life the way his hunting dog, Layla, chased a bird. Now he had come full circle. He was done. It was time to move back to where he would have space. He wanted land, trees, and a creek on his property.

Russ's exit plan was for Don to buy half of his shares in the company, worth $75,000, and for Don to pay him in monthly installments. Russ would sell his other half to longtime, trusted employee Jim Conyne, who had been doing the bookkeeping and dispatching in recent years.

Don knew his uncle loved him, but Russ still treated him as a kid. He liked to reiterate how Don's road from Rainier Beach to the University of Washington and on to Genesee had been well paved. "Hard work. That's how we built this business," Russ would say. But Don was fine with the arrangement. He was young—only twenty-six. Buying into a company at his age felt like a big step.

Gordon hadn't talked much about retirement, and Don was happy about that. He liked having him around. Gordon didn't have the meddling type of personality. He let Don have space to make some decisions without questioning his judgment as much as Russ had. But even though Gordon wasn't ready to retire, with Don's increased involvement, he did take more opportunities to be away from the office. Gordon and Katie had just gotten back from visiting the old Clark family farm in Leduc, Alberta, when Gordon pulled up a chair to his desk and sat down as he did every so often to catch up with Don.

"Anything new around here?" asked Gordon.

"Oh, not really. How was your trip?" His dad had been talking about getting his mother up to see the old farm for years—ever since they'd found oil in Leduc.

"Well, it was a wonderful trip. The Lees still own the old farm, so they showed us around. They've done quite a bit of work to the old house, the roads are paved now, and the town has grown. So it looked different, but it felt the same in other ways. Took me back in time. It's such a different life there. Saw my mother's grave, too," said Gordon, his voice cracking a bit.

Don didn't know much about his grandmother, Annie— really only that her death had been really hard on his grandfather Si, and that soon after that, they had sold the farm and left Leduc.

"I wasn't expecting I would get so emotional seeing her grave again," Gordon continued, his voice somber. "As soon as I saw her name, Annie Fair Clark, I broke down and cried like a little baby." He chuckled a bit now, explaining how silly he must have looked. "It was uncontrollable. I just remembered the four of us—my dad, Russ, Ray, and myself, burying her, and it just brought back a flood of tears I didn't even know I had."

Just a few months after Russ retired, Gordon would make a business decision that would—although he didn't realize it at the time—initiate a change in the trajectory of the company.

The negotiations to buy Emil Carl Fuel had started before Russ retired, but Gordon had been driving the deal all along. Emil Carl owned a similar but very small local fuel company on Rainier Avenue and Holly Street. He had been supplying Hillman City and its surrounding areas since 1907 and was ready to retire. Emil thought his only son would take over the business, but he wanted to be an accountant instead, so Emil looked to Gordon.

Gordon and Emil were friends, even though they essentially competed for both heating oil and coal customers. But Gordon found friendship in everyone. He never had any animosity toward anyone, even in direct competition for business. Emil knew Gordon took care of his customers the way he did himself, and since Gordon's son was now in the business, he knew Genesee was the company he wanted for his customers.

Emil's business was small, so just as Gordon had done in buying Genesee Coal & Stoker in 1929, he and Emil financed it themselves, on the foundation of friendship and a handshake, without going through a bank. Genesee Fuel agreed to pay monthly installments to Emil Carl until paid in full over the course of two years.

The new-customer deliveries began right away. But in an effort to maintain consistency and to avoid confusion for Emil's previous customers, Genesee driver Frank Richmond started making those deliveries in the newly acquired Emil Carl Fuel truck. The transition that winter was so seamless, customers often waved from a distance to Frank and said, "Hello Emil," or, "Thanks for the delivery, Emil." It wasn't until after this acquisition that the Clark men realized what a key role similar acquisitions would play in their company's future.

But the purchase of Emil Carl Fuel wasn't the only major event of 1963. For Don, it was turning out to be a year of multiple transitions. Anita hadn't planned on going back to work after Leslie was born. But times had changed in the ten years since her college counselor had told Anita that the only professions for women were teaching and nursing. Women were gaining a voice and choosing other professions, which had resulted in a shortage of teachers. The World's Fair had also flagged Seattle as a vibrant, modern city. Boeing was hiring faster than houses were being built. New neighborhoods were springing up east of Seattle in Bellevue and Mercer Island. With those new neighborhoods came brand-new schools and thus, a need for more teachers. The district begged Anita to come back, and finally, she said she would.

Don supported her decision. He knew she was a good teacher. She was respected by her peers, and her students had showered her with gifts and thoughtful notes at the end of every school year, which made him proud. Figuring out what to do with Leslie, who would be turning one year old at the start of the new school year, was easy. Anita's mother, Mary, was willing and very capable of taking care of her. Anita would drive Leslie to her mother's house, head to work, then pick her up on her way home.

To Don, this seemed to be the ideal scenario. Having his own mother help out with Leslie was not even a conversation. Katie had been receiving electroshock therapy every eighteen months, and that was helping. When she was in a good mental state, she was happy, loving, and adoring of her granddaughter. Her eyes twinkled when she watched her, but she was nervous to hold her, let alone take care of her. That, they all knew, would be too much for her. Any amount of responsibility for someone else would cause stress, worry, and anxiety that Katie didn't need. She herself still needed taking care of. Her condition was probably in some ways a result of her having had to take care of her siblings at such a young age and having no one to take care of her after her mother died.

While going back to teaching and taking Leslie to her mother's felt like the right thing to do at the time, by mid-October, Anita was coming unraveled.

"I'm just having a hard time focusing on my students when I'm thinking about Leslie—wondering what I'm missing. I feel like I'm not being a very good teacher, but I'm also not being a very good mother. I know she is in loving arms, but I can hardly wait for the bell to ring so I can go get her," said Anita to Don as they watched Leslie sidestep around the coffee table.

"Well, you don't need to work. I make plenty of money. Seems like it would make things simpler if you stayed home," replied Don as he glanced around the room. He liked things tidy. Small piles of clutter around the house were tolerable for a little while, but he noticed things were less picked up since Anita had gone back to work. Times had been stressful at work. If she were home taking care of the house, then he wouldn't have to worry about that as well.

"It seems like more trouble than it's worth," said Anita with a look of relief. So at the beginning of December, Anita gave notice that after the holiday break, she would not be coming back to work as she would be staying home with Leslie.

By February of 1964, Don had been faithfully making his payments to Russ on time as usual. He didn't like to be late for anything. But he also wanted to impress on his uncle that he could be trusted to run the company. The winter had been cold and snowy, which meant that for Don, who was still settling in as business owner, it had been a demanding winter.

It was an unusually warm Sunday afternoon on February 4, 1964. Don and Anita were expecting a visit from Don's parents. Gordon had just picked up Katie from the psych ward after another round of electroshock treatment. Don watched as his dad helped his mother out of the car, Gordon's gentle touch evidence of his constant care for her. Katie flashed her biggest smile and chuckled at the sight of her granddaughter toddling in her pajamas. Everyone seemed to be in good spirits.

While Leslie entertained Katie and Anita, Don and Gordon escaped to discuss matters at "the shop," as they called the business. Spring had seemingly arrived early this year. Normally this wouldn't be cause for celebration in the heating business since February is normally a cold month—good for sales. But this early dose of warm weather felt different. It seemed like a sign of good things to come. Don had made it through his first year filling Russ's shoes, and the company had completed the purchase of its first acquisition.

Katie seemed to be in a better place now, too, though right after her shock treatments, she was often a little confused. She seemed happier, but she also needed to be reminded of certain things. It was almost as if some of her recent memories had been erased. This had become a cycle. After a treatment, she would be slightly foggy and confused for a short time, then better for eight to ten months. Then over the next twelve to eighteen months, she would slowly revert back to her depressive state, and the cycle would repeat. It worried Don, but his dad was handling it, and that gave him so much comfort.

Throughout all this, his dad never complained about Katie. He just took care of her in a gentle, loving way. He drove her to doctor's appointments, arranged for her friends and family to visit, and hired help around the house. Although Gordon had had a few health scares himself and continued taking medication for the trouble with his heart, his focus was on Katie's health, not his own.

When it was time for Gordon and Katie to go after their visit, Don watched his parents leave the warmth of his house and drive into the damp, dark evening. Don shook his head and sighed. "Well, she seemed all right this time. Don't you think?"

"She seemed just like your mother," replied Anita. Don's mother had been depressed as long as Anita had known her. Don knew Katie wasn't the easiest mother-in-law, but he also knew Anita loved her despite her difficult side. "She'll be all right," Anita added.

Within an hour after Gordon and Katie drove away, the phone rang. Don answered and an unfamiliar voice spoke.

"Hello, is this Don Clark?" the woman on the other end of the line asked.

"Yes, this is Don."

"Well, your dad's been in an accident," she said. "Your mother seems OK, but we called an ambulance for your dad."

As soon as he got an address, Don jumped into his 1963 Chevy Impala and sped to the location of the accident. He pictured the worst, and as he approached, the sight of his dad's 1960 Cadillac Coupe de Ville on the side of the road didn't bring relief. It was sitting at an uncanny angle, crashed against a stacked rock embankment.

Lights from two police cars lit up the dark February sky. The policemen walked around the Cadillac, peering inside with flashlights. Buttoned up in her wool tweed coat, her bonnet still tied around her chin, Katie stood looking dazed and confused next to the kind neighbor who had phoned Don.

"The ambulance is taking your dad to Virginia Mason Hospital. It looked like he had a heart attack." The policeman walked with Don toward his fragile mother.

Don suddenly felt a heavy weight of responsibility descend on his shoulders. His mother appeared to be holding it together, but he never really knew how she was doing in any given moment. One thing was sure: it didn't seem like a good idea, given her mental state, to take her to the hospital. Not knowing what else to do, he drove Katie over to his cousin John Ward's house nearby, before heading to Virginia Mason himself.

At the hospital, they confirmed his biggest fear. Gordon had gone into cardiac arrest and died in the ambulance on the way to the hospital. He was 61 years old, and Don, 27.

Almost six years after the day his Uncle Russ had handed him a broom at work, Don had become majority owner of the family business and sole caretaker of his mother. His dad had been his rock and the voice of reason, always accepting and never judging him. Gordon had taken care of everything. He'd made complicated situations easier, had transformed chaos into calm, and had simply done whatever needed to be done. Devastated, shocked, and not sure how he would go on without him, Don felt paralyzed.

CHAPTER THIRTEEN

1964–1967

---

*There are men and women who make the world better just by being
the kind of people they are. They have the gift of kindness or
courage or loyalty or integrity. It really matters very little whether
they are behind the wheel of a truck or running a business or
bringing up a family. They teach the truth by living it.*
—JAMES GARFIELD

IN A STATE OF SHOCK, DON DID WHAT HE NEEDED TO DO
regarding funeral arrangements. Although he felt as if he
could hardly breathe, he had to hold himself together in front
of his mother. Katie's doctor assured him that her most recent
treatment would help her to deal with this staggering loss as
well as anyone could. Don hoped and prayed this were true—
that she would be all right. He didn't know the details of how
his dad had cared for her, and now she was his responsibility.

Gordon's family weren't the only ones feeling his loss. The
Rainier Valley of Seattle still felt like a small town in 1964, as it
had on that day in May 1929 when Gordon, Ray, and Si arrived
and decided to call it home. From day one, Gordon had started

building relationships with the area's business owners, leaders, and members of the community. It was obvious just how many people had known and loved Gordon when more than a hundred cars joined the procession from the funeral home in downtown Seattle to the Evergreen Washelli Cemetery in North Seattle. For Don, the experience was both heart-wrenching and heartwarming at the same time.

Days after the funeral, knowing he needed to get back to work but still feeling heavy with loss and grief, Don sat at his desk and contemplated his situation. He was no longer the kid who was joining the family business. He *was* the business. The reality of that hit him hard. *A business owner.* That was something he'd always wanted, but this wasn't the way he had envisioned it would happen.

Bruised and battered as he was, Don still had a job to do. In that moment he wished he had a business partner, a co-leader, or even a sibling, as his dad and Russ had had in each other. There in the office, though, he only allowed himself a few moments to wallow before telling himself to "get a move on," as his dad had often said to him as a kid, when he needed to get to the task at hand.

Not having a business partner did have its benefits. Don knew that. He had watched his dad and uncle for years. Now, whether he felt ready or not, it was his turn to make all the decisions and his opportunity to steer the business in the direction of success. He knew he could do it. It was what he had gone to college for. It was what he'd really been preparing for his whole life.

Pushing aside his grief and lingering self-doubt, Don straightened in his chair and grabbed his clipboard. When he was thinking, he had a habit of biting his pencil until the yellow paint cracked away, exposing the wood and forever changing the pencil's texture. Deep in thought, he'd already transformed one new pencil from geometrically smooth and yellow to dimpled, now freckled with tan half-moons. He released the pencil from his teeth and put its tip to the notepad in his first effort toward taking control of the daunting situation.

Making lists made Don feel productive. It was how he organized his daily plan, envisioned his weekly to-dos, and parceled his long-term goals. It was how he brought control to the overwhelming number of tasks that needed to be done. Don generally made two categories of lists: office and personal. Once he'd completed a task, he crossed it off with multiple lines—not just one clean line—because every accomplishment needed an exclamation point. That felt good. As soon as the list began to look messy, even if all the tasks were not yet complete, he tore off the page and started a new one, transferring the unfinished tasks to the new list.

One item on Don's list he never defaulted on was sending Russ the agreed-upon payments for his share of the company. Gordon had instilled in Don this trait—to always be prompt in payments. Don could hear the echo of his dad's voice: *If you owe someone money, you pay up, on time, every time.*

Not only did Don make his payments to Russ promptly, he also always included copies of the quarterly financial reports.

Fully retired now and no longer involved in the company's operations, Russ never asked for these reports, but he looked them over anyway.

Every once in a while, when he was in town for one reason or another, Russ stopped by the office. Always unannounced and always in through the back door and out through the front was his usual routine.

"Well hello, Uncle Russ." Don perked up as Russ made his way to his usual chair inside the door of Don's office.

"Donnie, how's business?" It was more of a rhetorical question since he already knew the answer.

Then, almost as abruptly as he had entered, Russ stood up and walked out. It occurred to Don that it had to be hard for Russ to come to the office now that Gordon had passed. Russ's and Gordon's lives had been closely intertwined, and Russ must have missed his brother terribly. Don also realized that this sudden walk-out—classic behavior for Russ—was metaphorical. Don was on his own, just as he'd known he was.

Gordon's brother, Uncle Ray, had remarried a few years back but never had children. He and his wife Mary now lived in a house that happened to be on the path Don took daily to collect the mail at the post office. When it came to Ray, Gordon had always been the brother who'd kept tabs on him. Now that Gordon was gone, it wasn't Russ but Don who stepped up to be there for him. Unfortunately, Ray was only able to kick his habit of drinking for short periods of time. As those habits usually go, every time he picked it back up, it got worse. Ray still worked as a fish broker, but Don wasn't sure how he managed. More often than not on his way to fetch the mail, Don saw Ray out on his front porch, well into his daily drinking at eight thirty in the morning. On the morning that would be his last, Mary called Don before she called the medics. He had collapsed in his driveway. By the time they all arrived to help, Ray was gone. He'd suffered from a fatal stroke at age fifty-three.

To Don's surprise, Katie was managing much better than expected in the year after Gordon's death. She lived within a mile of the office, so Don checked in on her daily. She couldn't drive but had learned how to take the bus to get her groceries. Since she had plenty of space in the house in Seward Park, she often let relatives or church friends stay with her for long periods of time, free of rent.

By spring of 1965, more than a year after Gordon's passing, natural gas had been a dirty word for nine years. In that amount of time, the heating oil industry had gone from owning 90 percent of the residential heating business to 65 percent, and natural gas's growth didn't appear to be slowing down. Subsidized by government funds, Washington Natural Gas was a monopolizing giant. Their iconic neon-blue flame lit the sky on Mercer Street, and TV advertisements sold viewers on gas's money-saving efficiency. When new neighborhoods went up in the suburbs, new pipelines were laid down. All businesses that relied on oil heating, as Genesee did, were still threatened by this industry disrupter.

Genesee worked hard to gain one new customer for every

one lost to natural gas. But the company had a difficult time keeping up, and it certainly wasn't growing. Through sales efforts, Don managed to attract new customers, but these were already-existing heating oil customers who'd been with other companies. As the popularity of natural gas grew, the heating oil industry as a whole was shrinking.

The problem was becoming a recurring nightmare. Don lay awake at night worrying about his future. He wished the answer to his current competition problem could be as simple as what his dad and uncle had done: just add the product that the competitors were providing. Looking back, it seemed like such an obvious solution. But he remembered the way Gordon and Russ had agonized over the decision, which he'd noticed, even as a ten-year-old. Change was hard, and it was also messy.

Don's dad and uncle had to spend more money during uncertain times, work harder without knowing where those efforts would lead, learn new procedures, and work out all the various problems that had resulted from the change. But they did it. They pivoted in response to the changing culture. By doing that, they re-created themselves and positioned themselves to survive long-term.

Don knew he needed to do something, but he wasn't sure what. He realized he needed to adapt to what was happening outside the company. He needed to change his strategy. If he didn't, the fate anticipated by Russ and Gordon would come true—it would be the end of the business.

While Don stewed over this situation at the office, happier matters were transpiring at home. On April 15, during that spring of 1965, Don was pacing inside the Swedish Hospital waiting room when a doctor came in and slipped off his mask.

"How is it?" Don eagerly asked.

"Well, it's not an *it*, it's a boy!" replied the doctor.

Don had a daughter and now a son. He hadn't expected how strongly his emotions would overtake him. In that moment, he felt both joy and sorrow. He wept. He didn't know if it was out of joy for this healthy boy and the start of his own father-son relationship, or if the deluge of emotion had resurfaced the loss of his father. Don was the only son of Eli Silas Clark's lineage. Now he had a boy—Steven Todd Clark—to carry on the Clark name.

With Anita and the baby staying at the hospital for several days, Don headed back to the office. Now this company was not only his livelihood; it was his legacy, one he wanted to carry on. He knew now that seeing Genesee into the future was his destiny. Yes, the industry was taking a hit, and the punches would continue for at least the foreseeable future. But he had to figure out a way to propel this business forward.

Don knew he couldn't just jump to a different product, but he *could* change his approach. Don's thoughts took him back again to when the company had bought Emil Carl Fuel, that small but significant acquisition. *That's it*, he thought. *That is how I will get this business to survive.* Buying other heating oil companies was the only way to grow. As an industry, heating oil customers were lessening, but *his* customer base could increase. He just had to absorb his competitors. This strategy might not work forever, Don reasoned, but as long as there were at least some heating oil customers in Seattle, Genesee could be the company to serve them.

Although Gordon and Russ weren't physically there to guide him, they had already shown him how to do what he needed to do. Don had followed their lead in maintaining good relationships with other business owners in the industry and by participating in associations such as the Rainier Valley Merchants Association and the Oil Heat Institute of Western Washington. Through those channels, heating oil company owners discussed strategies for battling the gas company and pooled their money for general heating oil television campaigns to increase awareness that "oil heats best."

Through the Oil Heat Institute of Washington, Don got to know Fred Griffin, of Griffin Fuel Company, and past president of the association. Quickly, Fred became an important force in Don's life. All the oil company executives looked up to Fred, as he was considered an industry patriarch—a leader with good business integrity. Don felt an immediate kinship with Fred, who was a fellow University of Washington graduate as well.

Building business relationships wasn't a stretch for Don. It came as naturally to him as it had to his dad. Although Genesee Fuel now had an exclusive contract with Shell as its oil distributor, representatives from Arco stopped by often, hoping to steal Genesee's business from Shell. Don found conversation easy with the Arco representatives, Dan Ledbetter and Harold Everett. He shared with these like-minded, forward-thinking men his business aspirations of growing the company by buying other local oil companies. Through conversations such as these, Don was positioning himself as the young, smart businessman with upward potential in the industry.

These connections paid off quickly. Late in 1965, Arco approached Don with an incredible offer. Bladine and James, another Seattle oil company, was for sale. Bladine and James was an Arco customer, and Genesee a Shell customer. But because Dan Ledbetter and Harold Everett wanted to work with Don, Arco sweetened the deal. They agreed to finance the whole amount of the sale if Genesee would sign a contract to do business exclusively with Arco instead of Shell. It was an opportunity he couldn't refuse.

Within days Don received a check from Arco for the full purchase amount. In further negotiations, Arco stated that if Don agreed to a long-term exclusive contract, the company would forgive half debt of the sale, meaning Don would only have to pay back 50 percent of the value. Opportunities like this don't happen often, and he knew it.

Don wasn't the only one making moves in 1965. The local economy was thriving. Seattle had reached a new peak population of 565,000. With air travel in the United States having doubled over the last five years, Boeing was cranking out jets and attracting out-of-state transplants for its new employees, who often landed in the suburbs. As the suburbs grew, the population inside the city began to decline. Even people who were already established in city neighborhoods found the wide streets and two-car garages of the suburbs to be more attractive.

One day in spring, Don sat on the couch, shoes off, one

sock dangling from the end of his foot, reading the evening paper. Steve toddled into the room while Leslie colored at the kitchen table. As soon as Anita had cleaned up the dinner dishes, she joined Don in the living room.

Don put the paper down to look at her. "You know, my dad used to say that when they first moved to Rainier Valley, his dad Si liked it because it felt like a small but growing town. He said the atmosphere reminded him of Leduc when he settled there. Seattle doesn't feel that way to me right now. It doesn't have that community feel like it did when we were in high school. What do you think about moving?" Don felt pretty comfortable financially now, since Genesee's customer base had doubled after the Bladine and James acquisition. He also liked the idea of a two-car garage.

"If we're going to move at some point, it would be nice to get settled before Leslie starts school," replied Anita. Leslie would be going to kindergarten in a little over a year. The Seattle school district had been dealing with lawsuits and changing politics surrounding desegregation. Anita's teacher friends felt discouraged and frustrated and believed that they were having less and less of a voice in a district that was constantly fighting battles.

Education was important to both Don and Anita, so it was decided that they would move just across the bridge to Mercer Island, a small city with its own public school district. But instead of buying a house, they bought a lot in the newly developing Parkwood neighborhood for $8,000.

Finding a builder was easy; it would be Anita's brother

Nik. A returned veteran and now general contractor, anything Nik put together was built with the greatest amount of thought, precision, and high-quality craftsmanship.

Finding an architect wasn't hard for Don either. Just as his dad had loyally done business with his customers, Don regularly did, too. If a car dealer was a customer, he'd buy his car from them. If a gas station owner was a customer, he'd go out of his way to buy gas from them. One of his loyal customers, George Lucker, was an architect, so naturally, Don turned to him.

Fortunately, George was good at his job. Not long after plans were already drawn, Don and Anita made a major change request. Their three-bedroom house needed to become a four-bedroom. Anita was expecting another baby. Karen Lee arrived on September 22, 1966, and six months later the family of five took occupancy of their new home on Mercer Island.

In a little over two years, Don had gone from being an employee of his dad and uncle's business to majority owner. In that same amount of time, he'd taken a shrinking business in an industry marked doomed, and more than doubled its size as well as its profits. Don even surprised himself by how well he was doing. But he was cautions not to let himself get too comfortable. He knew he couldn't count on things going this well forever.

CHAPTER FOURTEEN

1967–1973

If you can't fly then run, if you can't run then walk, if you can't walk then crawl, but whatever you do you have to keep moving forward.
—MARTIN LUTHER KING JR.

AT THIRTY-ONE, DON HAD REALIZED THE AMERICAN DREAM: A wife and three children, a new house, and a growing business. He felt as though he had arrived. Now he just needed to keep hold of it all.

The problem with *arriving* was that the stakes were now higher. More assets meant more risk and more things to take care of. Now the thought of failure was even scarier to Don. As history had shown, the business he was in was highly susceptible to climate, economic, and cultural trends that were beyond his control.

But for the moment, anyway, Don was handling the pressure. The Bladine and James acquisition had proven pivotal for Genesee's wellbeing. But more than that, it was important because of how Don's colleagues now viewed him. This was the first major business decision Don had made on his own, and it tagged him as a leader within the industry. Soon he would step into the shoes of his mentor, Fred Griffin, as president-elect of the Oil Heat Institute.

Good timing aided Don's success and boosted his confidence. Between 1967 and 1969, the local economy flourished. Unemployment was low, and real estate values were climbing. Gasoline was about thirty-four cents per gallon, a sign that the cost per diesel barrel was low and a good thing for the heating oil industry. That meant Genesee could buy oil cheaply and sell it to customers at a fair, competitive price and still make a decent profit. Additionally, low oil prices meant it was only marginally less expensive for homeowners to heat with natural gas as opposed to oil. Consequently, the rate at which customers closed their accounts to switch over to natural gas lessened dramatically.

Just as Don reached a good place with the company, he and Anita were also feeling satisfied at home. Soon they settled into a church community at Mercer Island Covenant Church, where they began lifelong friendships. The neighborhood they had chosen for their dream house was filled with the families of lawyers, doctors, business executives, and housewives. Most of the women played traditional roles in the family, so Anita was in good company as she took care of the house and children while Don spent his days at the office.

A natural teacher, Anita carried that trait into motherhood. She encouraged TV shows that promoted good values, such as *J. P. Patches*, *Mister Rogers' Neighborhood*, and *Little House on the Prairie*. But she also made sure the television was turned off every evening at 6:30 while the family sat down together for dinner. The bedtime "tuck-in" routine included reading books, hugs and kisses, and their own version of the rhyme: "G'night, sleep tight, don't let the bedbugs bite. If they do, hit 'em with a shoe, and they'll come back another night."

Both Don's and Anita's childhood family lives had centered on their faith, but there were some differences as well. Anita's parents had always welcomed into their home anyone who needed a place to stay—strangers who came through their church or a friend of a friend who was down on his luck—and those in need were welcomed to live with them for an indefinite period of time. Both Don and Anita were raised on the principle that we are all God's children and worthy of love, respect, food, and shelter, but Anita's family took it one step further in putting their beliefs into action. This basic love and care for others spilled over into the way she approached strangers and treated people in general. It also filtered into conversations with her own family around the dinner table or at bedtime.

One day five-year-old Steve came home from school bothered by the way another boy was being treated. Mercer Island was a predominately white community, and this boy was black. While Anita tucked Steve in for the night, she told him, "You know, inside that boy is just the same as you. God loves him. And God loves you. God loves that boy just as much as he loves you. No more, no less. And that is the way you should treat him." These words were not just left there for Steve that night. They would be repeated many times, in many situations, with all the kids.

It was a busy time of life. Just as Don and Anita had gotten comfortable in their new house as a family of five, they found out they were expecting another baby. As an only child, Don relished having a big family. He remembered how much his father had loved being a grandfather, and envisioned how Gordon would have spoiled rotten his many grandchildren. Anita, too, viewed each pregnancy as a blessing, but the idea of a fourth child was overwhelming. It took months to adjust to that reality. In fact, it wasn't until late in the fall of 1970—when Anita was seven and a half months pregnant—that she realized she hadn't even told her family. One day after babysitting for Don and Anita's kids, their niece, Nikki Sue, went home and revealed a great surprise: Auntie Nita was pregnant again. Less than two months later, on January 4, Andrea Lynn arrived.

Not only did the family grow in 1971, but now it was Genesee's turn to grow again. When the owner of Seattle Diesel died, he didn't have any kids to pass his company to. Several industry folks wanted to buy the business and made good offers. But because Gordon had been a good friend to the owner, Jack Polson, and because Don was well respected in the industry, the opportunity to buy went to Genesee.

Don felt honored to be the first choice in buyers and humbled as he thought of his dad and how Gordon's emphasis on developing relationships had set Don up for this deal. But Don still had a few reservations about buying a company as big as Seattle Diesel. He worried about the future no matter how good things were in the present. However, this time his apprehension was warranted by the recent downward-trending economy.

Since the end of World War II, the United States economy had been in an upward trend. That entire trajectory started to change when in 1971 the federal government canceled funding for its order of Boeing's supersonic transport aircraft, which had promised to carry passengers faster than the speed of sound. This event triggered a string of Boeing layoffs in Seattle. At first, as with any historic economic events, people not directly associated with Boeing didn't understand that they, too, would personally be affected. But the trouble at Boeing started a ripple effect. Soon the whole country started to dive into recession. In Seattle, the recession was especially deep.

It was unsettling to watch, even for those who kept their jobs. Don remembered the sobering stories his dad and Uncle Russ had told of customers who'd been unable to pay their bills through the Great Depression and wartime. Though Genesee Fuel hadn't yet experienced severe consequences resulting from the Boeing layoffs, buying Seattle Diesel would more than double Genesee's customer base. In an unstable economy, this made Don nervous.

If Seattle went deeper into a recession, Don would have twice as many customers who might not be able to pay their bills. He was conflicted between taking a risk on growing the business and playing it safe, maintaining what he had.

In the end, Arco stepped in again. They wrote Don a check to cover the whole cost of the sale, contingent on Don's extending his contract with them, and only expecting him to pay back a small percentage of the value of the company. *Not* taking that offer would have been leaving money on the table. So he took the deal, buying Seattle Diesel in the summer of 1971. With every handshake, Don grew more deeply invested than he had ever imagined possible. Consequently, he also became more exposed to risk. Whichever way the local economy trended, his fortunes would move the same way.

As a bonus, with this acquisition, Genesee acquired many really good employees, bringing the number on the company's payroll up to twenty-four. Don felt the same good fortune Gordon and Russ had felt when they first bought John Scott's Service station and Genesee Coal & Stoker—he'd gotten a two-for-one deal. Now, with twice as many customers and new employees, Genesee would be set for success—as long as the climatic, economic, and cultural factors moved in its favor.

Unfortunately, just a few months after the Seattle Diesel acquisition, things did not move in his favor. The economy took an even deeper dive. By the end of 1971, Boeing had let go of 75 percent of its workforce—driving unemployment rates in Seattle to the highest in the country. Ironically, Don found himself in nearly the same situation his father and uncle had just after buying the company in 1929, when the stock market crashed. Although Don hadn't been alive then, he'd heard the stories and dreaded a repeat of those events.

Those who'd lived through the Great Depression were filled with fear that those grim days were back with a vengeance. The classified section of the *Seattle Times* bulged with ads as people tried to sell everything, including the kitchen table, in order to keep the kitchen sink. But whereas the less fortunate in the Depression era had congregated and created comradery in Hooverville, many of the desperate and unemployed from the Boeing Bust sought a more permanent out. Suicides and robberies increased. Seattle became known as a city in despair. Newspapers ran stories about the mysterious "D. B. Cooper," believed to be a victim of the Boeing Bust, who hijacked a Boeing 727, demanded a ransom payment of $200,000, then parachuted into the Washington State wilderness with the stolen money. Not everyone took such drastic measures, but everyone seemed to be looking for a way out. "Will the last person leaving Seattle—turn out the lights," read one 1971 billboard satirizing the mass exodus.

As despairing times raged in Seattle, Don counted every blessing. He was thankful for each paying customer, his industry partners, his house full of family, and the fact he had a college degree to fall back on if worse came to worse. Don wondered how his dad had talked himself through his worry and uncertainty during the most difficult years of the Depression and war.

Then, in 1973, an event occurred that brought Don to his knees. On October 17, members of the Organization of the Petroleum Exporting Countries (OPEC) banned petroleum exports derived from crude oil to the United States. Heating oil (also called diesel) is extracted and refined from crude oil. Panic didn't set in among the public right away. Not many people understood how this would directly affect them. But Don knew. This was horrible news. For him and everyone in the industry who depended on foreign oil imports, the embargo was a massive direct threat to their business.

Having recently more than doubled his customer base, Don was deeply invested in seeing this crisis resolved. It was the beginning of the heating season. No one had any idea what kind of winter was coming, but mild or harsh, it was imminent. Don had four thousand customers who needed heating oil, and OPEC had just cut the supply to the company off.

This is it, thought Don, dreadfully. *This is going to be the end. The end of the family business. The end of my career.* He'd heard his dad and uncle say those words so many times. But this time, it felt real, and it scared him to his core. Genesee's underground heating oil storage tanks were full, for the moment, but Don wasn't even sure if there would be enough in the tanks to get through the week.

This crisis created so many problems, Don didn't know where to begin. But he wasn't alone. Everyone wanted answers. The executive director of the Oil Heat Institute fielded an avalanche of phone calls from news reporters. Soon a press conference was scheduled. A meeting was called at the OHI offices on Dexter Avenue, gathering all the representatives from each local heating oil company.

Don, now president of the Institute, would need to be in front of the cameras. He would be the face of the industry. To get ready, his colleagues set up a mock press conference and tried to prepare an answer for every question they could imagine. The hardest part, Don knew, would be keeping his composure. He had to convince the public there was nothing to worry about. "I assure you, we will have enough heating oil for our customers." He practiced saying it over and over in various voices, trying to answer that question in a way that would exude confidence to the thousands of viewers who would be watching him on their television screens and hanging on his response.

On the day of the press conference, Fred Griffin, who was still Don's mentor, saw his worry and pulled him aside. He put a hand on Don's shoulder in a fatherly way. "Don, I know you're worried right now," he said. "It all seems really bad. But just remember, things are never as bad as you think they are."

It had been a long time since Don had received a simple phrase of encouragement. He wondered what his dad would have said to him in that moment of worry. Although Don was a long way from feeling that things weren't that bad, he did feel a sense of relief in that moment. He wasn't alone here. There were good people by his side.

When the press conference started, Don found himself surrounded by a dozen microphones belonging to the local news media. If the situation had been positive, he would have felt like a movie star. But he didn't feel like a movie star. He didn't even want to be there. He was more nervous than he'd ever been and could feel his blood pressure rising. He was far from confident in that moment, but confidence was exactly the act he needed to put on.

"Will there be enough oil to last through the winter?" A

reporter thrust his microphone in Don's face. Don knew how to answer that one. He'd practiced.

"It's not a time to worry. We'll have enough for our customers." Uncertainty coursed through his veins, but confidence came through his voice. Now more than ever it was important for Don to advocate for the industry. Assurance was what had gotten them this far in their battle to keep their customers from switching to natural gas. In the end, if a customer stayed with heating oil, their reasoning often boiled down to this: They felt loyal to a local, Seattle-born business. They had trust in this company that had delivered for so many years. They believed in the warmth heating oil had brought them, and they had faith in Don. Not only was Don attempting to ease the worry of his customers over the potential oil shortage, but he was also trying to restore confidence in people's perception of the industry that had been under attack.

"Mr. Clark." The King 5 news reporter looked at him with furrowed brows. "What happens if God turns against us and we have a record cold winter?"

Don felt momentarily stunned. This question took him by surprise. During their mock press conferences, he'd thought they had covered every question possible, but they hadn't practiced this one. Don fixated on the reporter's nose, which felt as if it was pointing right at him and saying, "Gotcha!" But suddenly Don had an answer, and the credence to go with it.

"Well, all we can do at this point is pray to God that we don't have a cold winter." That was the truth. Don knew that really was all he could do. It was the opposite of what he'd done his whole career, which was pray for a *cold* winter. "We'll have enough," finished Don.

With that, the table was turned. Now the reporter was the one without words.

CHAPTER FIFTEEN

1973–1976

A pessimist sees the difficulty in every opportunity;
an optimist sees the opportunity in every difficulty.
—WINSTON CHURCHILL

HAVING ENOUGH HEATING OIL TO GET THROUGH THE WINTER was a major problem, but Don also had another problem. In addition to the shortage of oil, there was a shortage of gasoline, a fraction of which was extracted from crude oil and consequently now also rationed. Genesee was a business that depended on delivering its product to customers. Now not only was the product it needed to deliver becoming scarce, but so was the fuel for its transportation.

Public fear about this issue was palpable. Cars were a symbol of status and power, but now the freedom to drive them was threatened. Day after day, even hours before sunrise, cars lined up at the gas pumps. Streets looked like parking lots as lines of cars wrapped around corners. And once their tanks were filled, people still felt fear, even resorting to buying locks for their tanks to prevent thieves from siphoning their precious gas.

In late November of 1973, at the height of the Watergate

scandal, President Nixon finally diverted his attention from his troubles to address what was happening. Positioned in front of a blue curtain backdrop and seated next to the American flag, he reiterated via televised address what most Americans already knew: "We have an energy crisis." He then announced his six-step plan to combat the crisis.

Glued to the television, Don hung on every word, but his blood pressure rose considerably when he heard the president say, "There will be reductions of approximately 15 percent in the supply of heating oil for homes and offices and other establishments. To be sure that there is enough oil to go around for the entire winter, all over the country, it will be essential for all of us to live and work in lower temperatures. We must ask everyone to lower the thermostat in your home by at least six degrees so that we can achieve a national daytime average of sixty-eight degrees." The president tried to ease the pain by adding, "Incidentally, my doctor tells me that in a temperature of sixty-six to sixty-eight degrees, you are really more healthy than when it is seventy-five to seventy-eight, if that is any comfort." For Don, it was not a comfort. The president's words were a knife to his livelihood.

Just a few years earlier, Don had been worried about natural gas and how that utility was taking away his customers right and left. Ironically, now both the heating oil and the natural gas industries had the same problem: the energy crisis was causing the threat of shortages of both—since natural gas is a byproduct of the process of drilling for crude oil—and driving prices for both up exponentially.

But for some reason, the policymakers didn't see heating oil and natural gas as equal. After the president's remarks, the government clarified that only those who heated their homes with heating oil had to set their thermostats at sixty-eight. Natural gas users didn't have that same stipulation; they could turn up the heat as high as they liked.

This didn't seem fair. It didn't even make sense, since both forms of fuel would be held hostage by the crisis. Don had to do something. He had to be the voice for his customers and for the industry. Immediately Don, Fred Griffith, and a few other key players in the Oil Heat Industry got to work building a case to lobby on behalf of the oil industry. They took their petition to Washington, D.C., accompanied by their wives.

Don would testify in front of members of the United States House of Representatives Commerce Committee, including Washington State Representative Joel Pritchard and a United States senator from Washington, Warren G. Magnuson. Both Congressman Pritchard and Senator Magnuson had a strong allegiance to business in Seattle, and Don knew this.

Congressman Pritchard had grown up in Seattle's Queen Anne neighborhood, where a vast majority of the houses were heated by oil and supported the industry. Senator Magnuson was a graduate of the University of Washington and was known for securing remarkable amounts of federal funds for Washington State, including for the state's second World's Fair, the preservation and renovation of Seattle's Pike Place Market, and the establishment of the Fred Hutchinson Cancer Research Center, named after the Seattle baseball star who lost his battle with cancer in 1964 and whom Don had met on that house call with his father one Saturday morning in 1946.

Don stood in front of the panel. He was nervous, but it was the most incredible honor to stand in front of these decision makers. It had been years since he'd thought about the career he'd once contemplated pursuing. But ironically, had he chosen law school, he realized, he would likely not be standing there in that moment.

"Mr. Chairman," Don began. He took his glasses off and pointed them directly at Senator Magnuson, chairman of the committee. "Why do *some* Americans have to turn down their thermostats, but not *all* Americans?"

Don went on to explain that the shortage of crude oil meant a shortage of all products associated with its extraction: diesel, gasoline, and natural gas. Rationing and imposing penalties only on customers who used heating oil and allowing natural gas customers to be exempt was discriminatory.

Don's argument was solid, and the delivery superb. The Commerce Committee promptly agreed. Senator Magnuson affirmed he would see to it that the mandate to turn down the thermostat would pertain to all Americans. The petition was a success. Although it didn't change anything for his customers, it was a win for the industry on the principle of fairness during a time when Don and his peers felt as if nothing was leaning in their favor.

Later that evening, Don, his colleagues, and their wives had a celebratory dinner at the Kennedy Center. Congressman Pritchard joined them, and Don felt privileged to have the opportunity to talk to him one-on-one. What Don would re-member most about that conversation over dinner was Pritchard's unpretentious awareness of his position as an un-derdog Republican in the majority Democratic House. On a personal level, Pritchard also spoke fondly of his cabin on Bainbridge Island, a short ferry ride across Puget Sound from Seattle. Over the recent years, he mentioned, he and a few of his friends had invented the game of pickleball just to occupy their bored kids. Little did he know at the time, that sport would eventually be played in all fifty states.

Although Don still had a difficult job to do back at the office, he maintained his elevated mood the whole flight home. It was ironic that in the midst of such a terrifying time in his career, that experience in Washington, D.C., would be-come one of Don's proudest achievements.

But his exhilaration would not last. The trip to Washing-ton had been just one hurdle. There were still so many what-ifs. *What if we have a record cold winter? What if the supply runs dry? What if we can't get gasoline for the trucks?* Then Don heard his dad's voice echoing the words of Calvin Coolidge: "If you see ten troubles coming down the road, you can be sure that nine of them will run into the ditch before they reach you." Don hoped that would prove true, but he had his doubts.

Soon after returning from Washington, Don sat down at the oval family room table to the dinner that Anita served every night at 6:30. The kids found their specific places at the table and waited for their dad to say grace. Don took off his glasses, rubbed his face, and mumbled his usual prayer, all in one breath as a run-on sentence. "Heavenly Father we thank you for the food bless it to our bodies Christ's name Amen." As they started the "pass the potatoes" routine, Don made eye contact with Anita. They were about to have a serious conversation with the kids. They wanted them to understand that tough times were coming.

"Well, kids, things are going to be a bit tougher around here," Don began. "We're in an oil crisis. There's a shortage of heating oil, and it's going to affect the company."

No comments. Just the sound of utensils clanging on plates and serving dishes. Finally, Steve, now eight years old, broke the silence. "Does that mean I can't have cereal before bedtime?" Apparently, cereal was the luxury item Steve wasn't sure he could live without. Obviously, the matter was more serious than cereal, but this was an example Don could use to make his point.

"Well, that means we're not going to be able to spend as much money as we normally do." Silence followed. Steve gave him blank stare. "It might mean less cereal, but it also means less of everything." Don knew he had built a good life for his kids. His mother always said, "You give them too much. You're spoiling them." But his kids weren't growing up during a depression or a world war as he had. He wanted them to have more simply because they could. They did have a lot—brand-new bicycles, a purse full of Matchbox cars, and a membership to the Mercer Island Beach Club, where they could swim in a pool or in Lake Washington. For a long time now, they'd been able to afford those things. But would they forever?

When Don first bought into the business, he knew it was like buying a used car that would eventually stop running, as foreshadowed by his uncle and his dad. But Don had trusted his ability to make a used car go. When he got his first used car, as a teenager, he'd upgraded the tires and buffed out the scratches to make it look almost new. He also kept up on maintaining the engine but held on to some savings for the unanticipated breakdowns. He'd done the same with the business, using money carefully to improve and prolong the life of the company and also making sure to save enough for times of trouble, such as now.

But now, Don felt like Genesee was headed for a major crash. No one knew how long the fuel crisis would last, and he thought it very possible that the damage would be more than he could absorb. He looked at his kids around the dinner table, still silently trying to figure out what "less of everything" really meant. Don took off his glasses and rubbed his head, leaving his hair a mess. Then he picked up his fork and ate. He didn't have anything else to say. It was too soon to lay out the worst-case scenario. He wanted his family to know that things were not great in the business, but he didn't really want them to worry about what might happen. So he let the conversation go.

Later that night, and for many nights after, Don paced silently in his bedroom and up and down the hallway late into the night. Anita had been trying to keep everything else around him as normal as possible and in its usual order, but she was worried, too. While Don paced, Anita lay quietly in bed, eyes open, not sleeping either.

"Things will work out," she would say, trying to get him back to bed. "The crisis can't go on forever."

Don hoped this were true, but he *was* worried in a way he'd never been before.

Don wasn't alone in worrying for the industry. He found camaraderie with owners of the other local heating oil companies, as well as with the other businessmen in the Rainier Valley area. The Rainier Chamber of Commerce held meetings over coffee, and its members helped each other strategize how to handle the recent developments, including rising crime in the area.

Rudy, a Genesee customer and a Shell gas station owner up the road in Columbia City, had over the years taken care of all service problems Don encountered with his trucks. Because Don valued Rudy as a customer, he also always brought his personal cars to fill up at Rudy's station. Don saw Rudy's honesty and integrity in the way he ran his business. Now, when Don expressed to Rudy his worry about having enough gasoline to run his trucks, Rudy assured him he would. Somehow, Rudy would save gas for the Genesee trucks to fill up, even if his supply became dangerously low.

Rudy kept his promise, and Don was forever grateful. When he looked back years later, Don didn't know how Rudy was able to do that, or even if it was legal, but Rudy's loyalty and sacrifice had been a huge gesture of friendship—a friendship that had started as a business relationship.

While Don felt some relief from his worry after his conversation with Rudy, another concern rushed in. Following the law of supply and demand—the supply of oil being low and the demand high—the price per barrel had gone through the roof. Just as Genesee was heading into the coldest months of the year, heating oil prices tripled. The recession was starting to feel more like a depression. Tough times in Seattle were getting tougher. The number of "For Sale" signs around the city increased. In the worst cases, Don had seen two-by-fours nailed across windows and doors in high-end Seattle neighborhoods such as Mount Baker. He worried about customers being able to pay.

Don hated to raise prices for his customers, but he had no choice. If oil cost him more, he had to charge customers more, too. He lowered his margins as much as possible, allowing himself just enough profit to pay his employees, his bills, and his own salary. He remembered hearing about how Gordon and Russ had often gone without a paycheck during the Depression.

Besides the countrywide crisis, there was also trouble in the neighborhood. The Rainier Valley that had felt like home to Gordon and Si back in 1929 had changed. Crime had increased drastically. Local merchants who'd once stood tall, confident, and proud of their businesses were being driven out in fear. Sidewalk purse snatchings had increased so much that the elderly were afraid to walk outside, even in daylight. After three armed robberies within nine months, Rainier Jewelers closed its doors for good. Genesee Pharmacy owner Herb Tsuchiya dealt with his share of armed robberies as well. On one occasion, robbers broke through his floor, looking for drugs and money.

The way the Rainier Valley business owners supported each other was one reason Gordon had chosen to make the area his home and place of work so many years ago. That aspect hadn't changed. There was strength in numbers, and though increased crime had introduced an intense fear to the residents, a fight-or-flight reflex now kicked in. Merchants who refused to leave stuck together to fight, in a protective way, in support of each other. They simply would not be pushed out by crime. On January 9, 1974, the *Seattle Times* reported that when the police arrived at one particular robbery-in-progress, they found merchants from the surrounding stores armed with baseball bats waiting outside the store for the perpetrators to emerge.

Back in Gordon's day, he had been a member of the Rainier Businessman's Association. That group later became the Rainier Chamber of Commerce, and Don was now its president. In an effort to combat the increased crime, Don held monthly meetings and invited the Seattle police chief, Patrick Fitzsimmons. The business owners created a rotation of volunteers who painted out graffiti on Saturday mornings, and the police stepped up their presence in the neighborhood per Don's request. Don even allowed the police department access to Genesee's rooftop to give them a bird's-eye view of the drug deals that were happening on the corner of Genesee and Rainier.

Although these problems in the neighborhood felt big, for Genesee Fuel they were secondary to the problems caused by the embargo. The supply of oil and gas was still low, prices were still high, and Don still didn't know if his business would survive. Sitting on his couch one night, Don abruptly put his newspaper down and sat up to give the TV his full attention. President Nixon was once again addressing the country. Don held his breath, fearing more restrictions that would further hurt the business. "It is clear that the United States has entered a new era with regard to energy," the president said into the camera, "and as Lincoln once said, 'we must think anew and act anew.'"

On that day, President Nixon rushed into motion an authorization act that removed legal barriers and provided a financial incentive to the state of Alaska in order to start construction of the Trans-Alaska Pipeline. The pipeline would decrease US dependency on foreign oil by allowing crude oil to be transported from the oil-rich region on the North Slope of Alaska to the Port of Valdez, where it would be transported via barge to the mainland United States.

Just when Don had about decided the whole world was against him, finally President Nixon was giving him a glimmer of hope. It was optimistic news, and Don hadn't heard any in a while. If the new pipeline were going to help, that help was still years away—but at least it was something. The future of the business was still at stake, as was Don's livelihood, but good news seemed hard to come by those days. Here was a piece of it he could hold on to.

Yet the worst was still to come. One night in January 1974, as Don left the office at his usual time, he encountered an even bigger threat than the energy crisis—a threat to his life.

A creature of habit, Don was always the last to leave the office—usually at 6:00 p.m. so he could be home by 6:30 for dinner. Those who knew him best knew he stuck to his routine like a lifeline. His weekday habits were so predictable, his coffee shop acquaintances would start to wonder if he didn't show up at his usual time. Saturday was car-washing day. (Don had no tolerance for dirty cars.) Sunday was church, which meant leaving at 8:15 a.m. sharp and sitting six rows back on the far-right side of the sanctuary.

Per his usual routine, Don opened the back door at six that night to leave for the day. January in Seattle was always dark, cold, and rainy, but that wasn't the sight that surprised him when he opened the door. On this night, right there in front him was the barrel of a gun, pointing at his chest.

"Open the vault," the man said in a voice that was nearly a whisper. Don looked from the gun to the whites of the man's eyes, just barely exposed in the space between the red cowboy bandanna pulled up high over his nose and the dark stocking cap that sat low on his brow.

After the moment it took to register the request, Don turned and headed back inside, toward the vault. As Don walked, he tried to remember the last time he had actually opened the vault. Although he was typically one of the first ones into the office in the morning, he almost never opened it. That daily task was left to his dependable office staff. It had been years—maybe a decade—since he'd rotated the dial.

The intruder pointed his gun right at Don's head while he stood in front of the walk-in vault. Don wasn't even sure he knew the combination. Fortunately, muscle memory kicked in. His shaking hand turned the dial, executing the combination on the first try. He was then pushed inside by the gun at his back. Don could feel the gunman's agitation as he took inventory of the vault's contents: two large filing cabinets full of customer documents and, sitting on the floor next to the cabinets, a safe about the size of Don's Magnavox television set.

"Open that one now." The gunman briefly pointed his gun at the smaller safe, then trained it in Don's direction. Obediently, Don started on that combination, once again pulling the digits from his long-term memory. Don knew what was in that safe, and he hoped the gunman would be satisfied.

And he was. The second, smaller safe held the cash that had been collected that day—about $800—by customers who had come into the office to pay in cash, rather than mailing in a check. The gunman quickly grabbed the money, stuffed it into his half-zipped jacket, then aimed the gun directly at Don, not letting him move toward the door. Moments later, the man closed the door of the vault, locking Don inside the four-by-five-foot, airtight chamber.

Don sat with his eyes wide open, although he could see nothing in the pitch-black inside of the safe. He stayed motionless, hardly believing what had just happened. He imagined the gunman running out the door. He listened for any indication that the gunman might still be inside the building. Then he waited a few more minutes, let out a small sigh of relief, calmly flipped the safety latch, and let himself out of the vault. Looking around to make sure the gunman was gone, he picked up the phone to call the police, who arrived within minutes.

Don went home that night late for dinner. Still in shock, he told Anita what had happened.

"It was the strangest thing," he said. "I felt so calm while I was opening that safe."

"Calm? Was he still pointing the gun at you?" Anita gave him a look that said *calm* was not the way she would have felt with a gun pointed at her head.

"Yeah, he was pointing the gun at my head. But I felt this strong presence watching over me. I shouldn't have been so calm, but I was. I felt an angel was with me. Even though the guy had a gun on me, I just knew I would be OK."

Anita's eyes welled with tears, as they easily did with many emotions, including joy and relief. Don felt emotional, too. They shared a tender moment, both understanding how differently things could have ended that night. But they hadn't ended badly. Don had a guardian angel who'd reassured him he would be all right. Going to bed that night, he actually felt less worried about the future of the business than he had in a long time. It seemed the angel was letting him know all the other difficulties he'd been having at work would also be all right.

The next day, it was business as usual at Genesee Fuel. The gunman was never caught, and the $800 cash never recovered. But Don had a different attitude every evening when he walked out the door. He'd made it through another day. He just had to keep moving forward. To keep doing the only thing he knew how to do. Then, a few weeks after the holdup, in March 1974, good news finally arrived. OPEC had lifted its embargo. Although to Don it felt like the energy crisis had gone on for years, six months after it had started, it was over.

CHAPTER SIXTEEN

1976–1979

Yesterday is not ours to recover, but tomorrow is ours to win or lose.
—LYNDON B. JOHNSON

BY THE END OF 1975, THE COUNTRY HAD BEEN THROUGH THE Vietnam War, Watergate, and the energy crisis, none of which had left Americans feeling very patriotic. But the United States would soon celebrate its 200th birthday as July 4, 1976, approached. With Independence Day festivities on the horizon, Americans from coast to coast rekindled their patriotism and joined the celebration. From fire hydrants to cigarette lighters, everything and everyone wore red, white, and blue in anticipation of the country's birthday.

Most of Don's worries about the business had been relieved when the embargo relaxed. Heating oil prices had come down to pre-crisis levels. Oil Heat Industry television ads emphasized the warmer heat and non-explosive nature of oil. Once again, Genesee and other companies in its space saw a wave of people replacing old oil furnaces with new oil furnaces, instead of converting from oil to gas.

Since Don felt a renewed sense of stability in his career,

the company, and the politics surrounding the industry as the bicentennial approached, he wholeheartedly joined in on the "spirit of '76." He loved American history, and since he no longer felt his job was on the line, he jumped at the chance to take his family to the center of it all: Washington, D.C.

Don had had his eye on Boeing's new 747 ever since its first flight in 1969. Especially attractive was the first-class cabin with its upper-deck lounge, accessible via a metal spiral staircase. If he were going to fly across the country, he imagined traveling there in style.

"If we fly one way, we can splurge on first-class tickets," Don said to Anita while she tackled a mountain of laundry.

"How would we get back? Hitchhike?" she asked, without cracking a smile.

"Well, I was looking at that new Chevy station wagon. We need a new car anyway. We could pick one up in D.C. and drive it back."

"Hmmm . . ." was the only response he got from Anita while she was busy folding the never-ending pile of clothes. She didn't mind road trips, but she had never driven across the country with four kids in the car. Soon enough she gave in, noting that the family could celebrate Don's fortieth birthday on the trip. Don never made much of a fuss over his own birthdays, and Anita thought he deserved a special way to celebrate. First-class travel, visiting D.C. for the bicentennial celebration, buying a new car, and taking a good cross-country road trip home would be the ideal vacation for Don.

With its swivel chairs, fixed coffee tables independent

from the seats, and plenty of floor space, the first-class cabin on the new 747 felt like real luxury. It had only been two years since Don had succeeded in his lobbying efforts to equalize the thermostat restrictions. Returning to Washington, D.C., put Don right back in that exciting time. He felt a rush of glory recalling his big career win and could not have been more excited to show the kids where he'd been and what he'd done.

Before leaving Seattle, Don had contacted U.S. Congressman Joel Pritchard of Washington State and scheduled a visit to his office. That day, as they made their way to the congressional office building, they were stopped on the sidewalk by a crossing guard allowing space for a big band that marched right down the middle of the street. Full of patriotism, Don grinned from ear to ear and swept the air with his arm, as if directing the band himself. After their visit and opportunity to shake hands with Congressman Pritchard, eleven-year-old Steve whispered to Karen, "Dad must be really important." Don overheard and beamed with pride.

A few days later, they picked up their new metallic powder-blue Chevy station wagon in D.C. and started their driving tour of Williamsburg, Virginia; Philadelphia; New York; Boston; and finally, Montreal, before heading west toward home. "Does everyone on the East Coast dress like this?" thirteen-year-old Leslie asked when they arrived in Williamsburg. Everywhere they looked, people wore 1776 period costume. It was as if they had stepped into a time capsule.

As they traveled from city to city, nine-year-old Karen sought out every hotel pool and gift shop and wrote about them in her journal. She also thought it particularly funny when, in Williamsburg, the family put her dad in the pillory, a wooden stockade enclosure that trapped his head and hands.

"Look, Dad's in jail!" Karen laughed, and the others joined in.

"Oh wait, let me take a picture." Anita got out her camera and snapped several photos of Don, alternately smiling and looking somber, as he played the part of prisoner.

"OK, get out of there now, Dad." Five-year-old Andrea was getting nervous. But nobody actually called her Andrea anymore. As a baby, she'd briefly been called Andy, but then Karen morphed the endearment to Nanny, and the rest of the family, neighbors, and school friends followed suit.

"Well, I can't. I'm in jail now, Nanny." Don played along, loving the theatrics and his audience of one.

"Dad, get out now! Get him out!" Nanny looked to her mom, panicked and near tears.

"Oh, it's all right, Nanny. Did you think he was stuck in there for good?" Anita opened the enclosure, letting the prisoner free.

Four weeks later, they started on a leisurely return trip across the country, toward home. The wagon was big enough for the six of them, as long as Nanny sat in the front seat between her parents. At an unscheduled stop, they stumbled upon Tommy Bartlett's waterski show on Lake Delton in Wisconsin, and there began Steve's fascination with waterskiing.

Jetted fountains danced to patriotic music while skiers in flashy red, white, and blue outfits made human pyramids, climbing on shoulders into formations three and four people high. The performers held American flags and waved to the audience in the grandstands as they passed by, then circled again to start the next trick. It was "The Greatest Show on H$_2$O," as titled, and turned out to be one of the most memorable stops and a welcome break to the hours spent inside the powder-blue station wagon.

Back on the road, Don and Steve entertained themselves by spotting and identifying trucks.

"Hey, Steve, look at that one. Is that a Mack Model R?" Don's head swiveled back and forth from the road ahead to the semi they were passing on their right.

Steve had already seen it coming. "No, that's a Peterbilt. Look at that grill. It's a Pete 358." Steve craned his neck, looking back as they passed.

It was a fun game to help pass time over three thousand miles on Interstate 90. But for Don, it was also reminiscent of the times he'd spent talking about cars and trucks with his dad, a passion that seemed to have been passed down through the male Clark genes, in addition to Steve's affinity for food.

At every restaurant they visited, the family found entertainment in challenging Steve to finish everything on his plate —including the garnish of parsley. Don sweetened the deal by adding a reward of fifty cents. On the verge of a growth spurt, Steve hardly needed any incentive, but he gladly took the challenge and, in most cases, earned his money.

On that long drive across the country, Don also did a lot of thinking. He looked at his kids and remembered himself at their same ages and how different his life was back then from theirs now. He looked specifically at Steve and noted their physical similarities—the straight blond hair, blue eyes, and slender build.

Moreover, Steve had a paper route, and he rode his bike all over his neighborhood in a ten-mile radius, just as Don had. Soon, Steve would start working at Genesee, at about the same age at which Don had started there. It would even be the same building and the same commute —twenty minutes in the car with his dad. But both the place they were coming from on Mercer Island and the place they were going in Rainier Valley were drastically different places in the mid-'70s than they'd been in the mid-'40s.

In Don's childhood, everyone had been affected by wartime, which not only brought fear, but also a sense of community and fellowship. People helped each other in whatever ways they could. Fear was of what lay beyond the country's borders. Although the recent bicentennial celebration echoed the postwar patriotism he'd grown up with, in general Don felt more community unrest. Instead of being in a foreign war, he thought, we were almost at war with each other. There was a greater divide then between the haves and the have-nots.

Don remembered the sizable gulf he had felt between himself and his own father when he was going off to college— a place so foreign to a Canadian farmer turned American businessman—and he vowed to make education and opportunity a priority for his kids.

⚜

Thirteen-year-old Steve liked working in the city at Genesee. Compared to his home on Mercer Island, the city was bigger, busier, with more unknowns, a little more danger, and a lot more sirens. Working there made him feel important and brave. He liked that it was recognizable yet diverse. Being outside the shelter and familiarity of the suburbs felt like an adventure. His dad paid him $2.50 an hour doing odd jobs around the building—picking up trash, cleaning windows, and things like that.

One week, Steve's job was to paint the awning out front, on the Genesee Street side of the building. Since it was a hot summer day, he wore a T-shirt and an old pair of shorts. As he stood on the ladder, he heard siren after siren, and watched police cars speeding past him on Genesee Street and nearby Rainier Avenue. From up high on the ladder, he could see beyond the radius of where he felt comfortable walking. It was exciting. He wondered if the cars were responding to a bank robbery or a murder.

An hour or so later, Steve got down off his ladder and headed to the Safeway on the corner of Genesee and Rainier to buy some lunch. He had been there a million times. The Safeway was in a nice new building. The parking lot was even bigger now, since the Genesee Stop Tavern—once a hub of drug-dealing activity—had been demolished. As Steve walked across the parking lot, he saw three police cars coming from different directions, all pulling into the same parking lot where he was walking. More excitement.

But when the three police cars rushed at him and blocked his path on every side, his thrill quickly turned to fear and then to panic as the car doors flung open and in a matter of seconds police officers had Steve surrounded.

"Where you going?" The officer held a hand on the pistol at his belt.

"Safeway." Steve motioned with his head, afraid to move any other muscle.

"Where have you been?"

"Just working. I'm working at Genesee Fuel. Just painting."

"Can anyone vouch for your whereabouts about twenty minutes ago?"

"You can ask my dad. He's the owner of the company." When he said that, Steve could sense the officers backing down. They must have realized his age, as they were looking for a guy in his twenties. A few seconds later, the officers told him to go on ahead. They explained that they had been looking for a five-and-a-half-foot Caucasian male with blond hair. Steve fit that description.

Later at the office, Steve didn't tell his dad what had happened right away. He'd gotten what he wanted from Safeway, and by the time he returned, he was no longer rattled. He didn't tell his dad because he didn't want him to worry. He wanted to keep working at the office. He was making good money—saving for a car—and didn't want the incident with the police to derail that.

A few months later, Steve noticed a commercial real estate sign on the front of the Genesee Fuel building that read, "Will build to suit." Feeling surprised, curious, and a little worried, Steve asked, "Dad, what's that sign for? Are you selling this place?" He had gotten to be very comfortable in and around the office. He was surprised at how nervous the thought of selling the company made him.

"Oh, no. We have a big piece of property. I'm just seeing if anyone wants to lease space, but it probably won't happen." Don went on to explain that if he could rent out a section of the property, he could generate some steady income that wasn't dependent on the weather or the state of oil. The Rainier Valley Chamber of Commerce was making efforts to improve the outlook of the neighborhood for businesses and customers, but still, Don couldn't find a renter.

Steve was relieved by that response. He liked his job at Genesee and felt proud that his dad was the owner. He pictured himself one day as a businessman, although probably not at Genesee. He thought maybe he'd end up working in a high-rise building somewhere downtown. But for now he liked being there and didn't want that to change.

By 1979, even though people were turning up their heat without reservation. Don still paid close attention to the world news. He knew politics and foreign relations played a significant role in the industry now. He read the morning paper at the Washington Athletic Club, watched the five o'clock news in his office, then read the evening newspapers on the couch at home. The 1973 oil embargo had left a scar. He remained cautious, with good reason.

Since 1973, foreign oil imports had dramatically increased

every year to a point in 1976 when the United States was consuming one quarter of OPEC's production. This was simply because people were consuming more products used daily that are made from crude oil such as candles, car tires, hand lotion, and even sweaters. In 1977, the Trans-Alaskan Pipeline was completed. Americans were pumping crude oil within their country's borders but still relied heavily on imports. Later that year, in 1979, a political uprising in Iran led to an Iranian revolution and war with neighboring Iraq, which brought on the threat of a second embargo. Once again, Don found himself back in the pressure cooker. Supplies fell short and the price of oil immediately spiked. Panicked car owners once again lined up at the gas pumps.

It had only been six years. The 1973 energy crisis—albeit short—was still fresh in people's memories, and no one wanted to relive that time. Americans were frustrated, losing hope, and patience. The patriotic confidence that had been re-energized during the bicentennial now fell flat. A telephone poll released in early May 1979 reported that over half of Americans believed the oil shortages were not even real but rather created by oil companies just to drive up prices. Don threw up his hands at that. People were pointing fingers, and it seemed as though no one believed in anyone or anything.

On July 15, 1979, President Jimmy Carter addressed the nation with what he called the "Crisis of Confidence" speech, although it was later referred to as the "Malaise Speech." Sitting behind his desk wearing a blue suit, he explained what he believed was the biggest threat to the American people. Bigger than a recession, bigger than unemployment, and bigger than longer lines at the gas pump; he thought something else was at the root of the problem.

"The threat is nearly invisible in ordinary ways. It is a crisis of confidence. It is a crisis that strikes at the very heart and soul and spirit of our national will. We can see this crisis in the growing doubt about the meaning of our own lives and in the loss of a unity of purpose for our nation. The erosion of our confidence in the future is threatening to destroy the social and the political fabric of America."

The president's frustration in a lack of coming together and in an overall decline in American values was evident. Americans had become wasteful. They drove their own cars when they could carpool or walk, they kept their thermostats up at night, and left their lights on all day. When threatened by the potential of a second shortage, people complained and placed blame on anyone except themselves. So, in the speech that was also a bit of a tongue-lashing, President Carter urged all Americans to "stop complaining and start conserving."

He went on to describe his plan to decrease foreign energy dependency and increase domestic independence. While Don agreed with President Carter's sentiments on lacking values and not coming together as Americans, he worried about the president's plan. He feared for his business: the supply, the prices, and what would become of his livelihood if his customers conserved too much.

One Saturday morning before dawn, Don walked the neighborhood, delivering papers on Steve's paper route. Steve was sick that day, so Don had offered to take his route. Up and down driveways he walked, nostalgically remembering his own paper route in Rainier Beach. Life had seemed so simple back then—even when he was a college graduate, a salesman, a Genesee truck driver, a new parent, a new homeowner, and then a new business owner. He might not have thought so at the time, but looking back now, life and the business had been straightforward, transparent, and uncomplicated.

As Don tossed the last rolled up and rubber-banded newspaper onto the last front porch to complete the paper route, he wished he could have that simplicity again. Back then, he didn't know what the future held any more than he did today. The only difference was that the stakes were so much higher now. He had built his life exactly how he had dreamed, but in doing so, he didn't realize that would mean he had so much more to lose. It seemed like such an unfair and unreal contradiction, but it was real. The stakes were high, the fear was deep, and the unknown was vast.

CHAPTER SEVENTEEN

1980–1993

Nothing in this world can take the place of persistence. Talent will not; nothing is more common than unsuccessful men with talent. Genius will not; unrewarded genius is almost a proverb. Education will not; the world is full of educated derelicts. Persistence and determination alone are omnipotent. The slogan Press On! has solved and always will solve the problems of the human race.
—CALVIN COOLIDGE

AFTER THE INITIAL PANIC, THE REALITY OF THE SECOND ENERGY crisis wasn't as bad as the first. Circumstances weren't entirely negative for the general population, although they did impact Genesee and its customers. This time the supply wasn't as big of a threat; the problem was that heating oil was expensive.

As a service to the customer, Genesee allowed customers to pay for their tank of oil in monthly budget payments. This was a practice that had begun informally during the Great Depression, with Gordon. Filling an oil tank was traditionally like filling a car with gasoline: once it goes into your tank, you buy it and it's yours to drive off with. In the case of heating oil, many more gallons are bought at once, so the price of a whole tank is much higher. It was often hard for a customer to pay for several months of heat upfront upon delivery of a tankful of oil. So Genesee allowed its customers to pay an agreed-upon amount per month over the course of the year, as a way to ease the pressure of paying one big bill at each time of delivery.

The problem with this scenario is that the price of heating oil fluctuates, so the agreed-upon amount was nothing more than a best guess. Under ideal circumstances, if the price fluctuated only slightly and the winter temperature was average, the monthly budget payments were enough. By the end of the heating season, the customer would have a zero balance heading into the next season.

During the energy crisis, however, the price of oil made a massive jump, but the agreed-upon amount per month for most customers had been based on their first delivery of the season, when prices were lower. When oil prices skyrocketed, the company had to start buying oil at the new, higher market price to make its scheduled deliveries. Since the customers were paying the original budgeted amount as set up months prior when the prices were low, it was now a problem because that amount wasn't enough to cover the cost.

Gail Herrmann, Genesee's credit manager, had the job of recalculating the payments and breaking the news to the customers. "Oh, hello there, Mrs. Jones. This is your oil man." Gail believed the tone of voice was important when making these calls. He had to be friendly and understanding, but firm and unwavering. "I am very sorry to bother you today, but you know the very prompt payment of twenty dollars per month you've always made is not quite covering the cost of the oil as it is today," said Gail. The customer needed to know their hardship was understood, but at the same time, the company needed to cover its costs. "Before we go into the new heating season, we'll need you to pay all of last winter, and then we'll have to raise that budget up to about seventy-five dollars per month." In most cases, if they were good paying customers, they understood, but sometimes they didn't, and Gail had to make it a little clearer. "Well, if you can't pay it up, it puts us in a tough situation," Gail reasoned. "It's like at Frederick and Nelson when you buy Christmas presents. They won't let you buy more if you haven't finished paying off last year's Christmas presents."

It was a constant battle throughout the early '80s as the conflict in the Middle East continued to drive oil prices up, infuriating customers and making it hard for them to afford heating with oil. Once again, customers started fleeing toward natural gas, and neither Don nor anyone else in the industry had an argument that would help.

Local heating oil company owners were tired of fighting, so if they could, they looked for a way out of the business altogether. This situation, however, presented Don with another buying opportunity: Seattle Fuel Company—a good, solid company, with a healthy customer base. Most heating oil companies at the time were locally, independently owned, but Seattle Fuel Company was owned by a corporation—Texaco.

Stan Rottrup, the Texaco representative in the area, had

gotten to know Don, both through his industry leadership and the fact that they shared a common faith. Stan was very involved in the First Covenant Church of Seattle, and Don was an active member of the Mercer Island Covenant Church. As a major corporation, Texaco had a long list of viable buyers for Seattle Fuel, but Stan Rottrup placed his trust in Don, shepherding him as a buyer.

The timing wasn't ideal. Since the first oil crisis, in the '70s, big oil companies were no longer willing to finance the deal as Arco had with Don's previous purchases. This one would have to be all on Don—the risk would be his alone. Oil prices were still high, and customer changeovers to natural gas still too frequent. But unlike Don's past purchases, where the goal was to grow the company, this one was less about growing and more about just staying in business. It was the early 1980s. Don still had kids to put through college, and he needed the business to get him through that.

At this point, Don wasn't sure if any of his kids would ever want to take over the company or if there would even be a company to run by then. But he felt an obligation to try and make it an option—either for them, for himself, or out of respect for his dad, uncle, and grandfather. He wasn't sure exactly which.

In terms of the family, Russ and Beulah were both gone now. Russ passed away of multiple myeloma in 1983, at seventy-eight years old. For months leading up to his death, Don had been making the two-and-a-half-hour drive that included a ferry ride to Port Angeles on the Peninsula of Washington every week to check in on them, but the visits were anything but pleasant.

While Russ fought off his cancer symptoms, Beulah suffered from dementia. In her confusion, she often forgot to feed the dog or let him outside to do his business. She complained that her ashtray was too full, spilling over with crushed cigarette butts, but she still lit up the next one, possibly forgetting she had just put one out. She blamed Russ for everything she didn't understand, which caused quarrelsome friction between the two of them.

Their decline was hard for Don to witness, but he knew it was his responsibility as Russ's only living blood relation. His uncle Russ had never really been a father figure to him, even after his dad died, yet Don had looked to him for approval for so many years, giving him the financial reports and relishing his praise. "The company wasn't making that much money when I was running it," Russ would say. In the end, Russ looked at Don with proud fatherly eyes.

Ironically, Don's mother, Katie, who had struggled with mental illness her entire adult life, was outliving both Gordon's and her own siblings as well. Don had continued taking care of her the way his dad did—monitoring her depression and alleviating it with shock treatments—but in general she had become a happier person once she moved into Covenant Shores Retirement Community on Mercer Island. Three of her four grandkids worked as table servers in the dining room there, and Katie finally developed a relationship with them—Karen, especially. Karen made an effort to stop by her apartment after almost every shift, even if it was just to sit and watch *Jeopardy!* with her for a few minutes.

By 1986, oil prices had come down again, and Don was able to exhale. Time marched on at home, and the kids were choosing their paths, which pleased Don. Leslie was twenty-three, had graduated from college, and was now married, living in Anchorage, and working as an interior designer. Twenty-one-year-old Steve was working toward a degree in business at Oregon State University. Karen, age twenty, was at the Culinary Institute of America in Hyde Park, New York, working to become a chef, and Nanny, fifteen, was the only one left at home and still in high school.

Don had always placed a high value on education. He had made it a goal to be able to pay for each of his kids' college education, wherever they chose to go. Although he remained loyal to his Washington Huskies—attending every home football game with Anita, a loyalty amplified by an extravagant tailgate with friends—he encouraged his kids to make their educations their own and to discover new places while they were both old enough and young enough.

It was another instance in which Don wanted to give his kids what he hadn't received as a young man. For him, going to college meant making a short commute to the well-respected University of Washington. But when it came to his own kids' educations, he encouraged them to go wherever they felt called.

In 1989, Don and Anita sat in a parent orientation meeting at the University of Colorado, where their youngest, Nanny (or Andrea, as she would be called after high school), would attend. "Happiness is when the last kid goes to college and the dog dies," Don said with a chuckle after introducing himself to the other parents in the meeting. Don was never far from a joke.

Although he would never stop worrying about his kids, having the last one launched meant that he'd accomplished what he set out to do: get them all successfully started in life. The pressure was lifted. Genesee had come through the fire unscathed, as well. The decision to purchase Seattle Fuel Company had been a good one, and, with the second oil crisis now over, the road ahead was finally looking clear. In fact, Don had grown the company to the point where it ran so smoothly he could spend less time at the office and more time out and about, traveling the world with Anita, as he'd always wanted to do.

It was now 1992. Steve wore a suit and parked his Porsche 944 in the parking garage of his high-rise building in downtown Portland, just a few blocks up from the Willamette River. The Porsche was, in part, a graduation gift from his parents. They'd agreed to buy him the car of his choice, up to a certain dollar amount. Steve's car of choice, even used, was over the budget. But Steve was determined, so he scrounged up the last of his savings and, adding it to the graduation money from his parents, bought a used Porsche 944 with sunroof in garnet.

The look suited him. His dirty-blond straight hair was long enough to flow in the wind when he had the sunroof open, but short enough for his businessman persona. He paid attention to the latest fashion, wearing Levi's 501 jeans and a T-shirt with a corduroy sport coat on top when he wasn't wearing a suit for work. He had a serious girlfriend he'd met in college and had the next few years of his life mapped out in his mind, which included marriage and buying a house.

Landing a good job in Portland, Oregon, the state of his alma mater, was ideal. Portland was geographically situated between high school Steve and college Steve, and it felt like an up-and-coming city for the young twenties crowd. A decade earlier, Portland had been like Seattle's little sister. Then between 1980 and 1990, the city just a few hours south of Seattle started to grow in population and popularity. In 1988, Nike, based in Oregon, launched their "Just Do It" campaign, and in 1990 opened its flagship retail store, Niketown, in the city. Portland had a vibrant, active, Northwest feel and a growing interest in microbrew. Steve felt right at home. Both physically and mentally, he was exactly where he wanted to be.

Like most new jobs, Steve's was a grind at first—a stockbroker at the Portland branch of Dain Bosworth, a big brokerage firm based in the Midwest. For a new broker, it was similar to starting a business, since he had to establish his client base before he could make much money. But it was an exciting time for him. He was in the grown-up world now and felt like he had so much potential.

While many brokers preferred working with the big Fortune 500 clients, Steve felt a kinship with small business owners. Having grown up under the umbrella of a small business himself, he understood them better than most and had become fascinated with their stories. Everyone knew that the executives at big companies were going to be financially successful, but no one had heard much about the small-company guys. What Steve found out was that some of the businesses that made the most money were the ones he would have least expected to do so.

One such client owned a welding supply company. Steve's job was to find out the man's net worth, in order to qualify him for an accredited investor. A welding supply company wouldn't have struck anyone as a high-rolling concern, but when he investigated, Steve discovered that this client was worth $6 million in 1990. He owned a twenty-person supply company, similar in size to Genesee.

In the months that followed, Steve started to question his direction in life and in his career. The novelty of his new job in this new city had worn off. He'd had a pretty devastating breakup with his college girlfriend, which left him feeling vulnerable, lonely, and a little homesick. Steve found himself thinking more and more about his goals in life and about where exactly home was for him.

One quiet Saturday morning, Steve picked up the phone and called his dad. He called him at the office, because he knew he was always in the office on Saturday mornings. In that conversation, Steve started asking questions about Genesee. At first, he felt his dad's enthusiasm over his sudden interest, but he also felt some hesitation.

"Why so many questions? Are you thinking you want to get involved in this business? What's the matter with the job you've got?" Don often jumped to conclusions.

"Well, no. I just have some small-business clients and it's just making me think about the family business, that's all," Steve replied.

"Well, it's been a good business for me, and it was for my dad, but it's a declining business now. You've got a good thing going in Portland. I would think you could make a really good living with that." That was the end of the conversation. Don was right. It had taken several years, but Steve was finally getting to the point where he was making good money.

Yet, Steve couldn't stop thinking about the family business and what his future might look like there. Time and time again, he came across clients with small family businesses that had been passed down through generations. There was something so special in those businesses. Their roots ran deep. Their products were simple enough to transcend generations, and the companies themselves were so American.

After having that conversation with Steve, Don started thinking nostalgically about the business that ran through his veins. The oil heat industry in general had continued to shrink, and quite frankly, Don was surprised he was still with it —or that the business was still with him. The end, as his dad and uncle had said, had gone on for more than thirty years, and it was still going.

Don felt fortunate to have done well in his career. He had never considered himself wealthy, but he had been able to maintain a modest house (the same one they'd built in 1964), live a modest lifestyle, and put his four kids through college, and he was setting himself and Anita up for a comfortable retirement. He really didn't see a viable future in the industry. But in thinking about his lineage and the sacrifices his grandfather and father had made, allowing him the opportunity to run the business, he was surprised to find it left him sentimental.

What Don wanted to do was stop worrying about the future of the business and coast into retirement. Or he wanted someone to make him an unsolicited offer to buy the business that he couldn't refuse. What he really didn't want was for one of his kids to feel obligated to step in just so the family business would remain in the family. He wanted to enjoy his golden years as his own father tragically was not able to do. But the question kept coming. "So, Dad, when you retire, what will happen to the company?" It popped up once more over Thanksgiving, when Steve was home for a visit.

"Well, I only have five or six more years to live anyway." Don was approaching the age at which his own father had died, and he was convinced he would have the same fate. Whether he really believed it or not, he said it often, perhaps more for the reaction he received.

"Oh, Don. Why do you keep saying that?" Anita had little patience for his cynicism.

"Yeah, Dad. Gramma is ninety. What makes you think you won't live that long?"

Although he made light of it, the underlying worry was there. "I was only twenty-seven when my dad died. Left me the company." Don shook his head, lost in thoughts about his father.

Steve was thinking about something else. That very moment it hit him: he was twenty-seven years old.

CHAPTER EIGHTEEN

1993–1999

There are many things in life that will catch your eye,
but only a few will catch your heart. Pursue these.
—MICHAEL NOLAN

THROUGHOUT THE NEXT YEAR, THOUGHTS OF THE FAMILY business kept invading Steve's thoughts. They were like a gentle tap on his shoulder. Most of the time he felt satisfied and secure in his job. When he was busy at work, he didn't notice or think much about Genesee Fuel, but over the weekends he couldn't ditch the feeling that he might be missing something. He finally initiated more serious conversations with his dad, who encouraged him to seek advice from others in the fuel industry.

Steve didn't have to look far to find someone whose advice he trusted. Jim Coon was a Portland acquaintance of Steve's through Young Life, a Christian organization for high school students that Steve volunteered for. Like Steve, Jim had grown up around his family oil business in the Portland area, and like Steve, he too had chosen a different route. Steve wondered if Jim had gone through the same thought process and wanted to know why he'd ultimately decided not to join the family business. He wondered if Jim had been relieved not to have gotten tangled up in it and whether he ever had regrets.

A few days later, Steve and Jim met for breakfast at the Bijou Café on Third Avenue in downtown Portland. Steve told him about the situation—that he was thinking about taking on the company, but that he had many reservations and wasn't sure if it was really what he wanted to do. He asked Jim if he had ever wanted to get into his family's business or why he hadn't. Jim hesitated as if he had to muster up a little courage to talk about it. He took a sip of his coffee, then explained that there had been a family squabble in the business that had resulted in Jim's dad selling the company out from under him years ago. Jim expressed his regret and sadness over the loss. He had wanted the business but wasn't given the opportunity, and now it was gone—out of the family.

"Steve, it doesn't matter if you stay with it as your career for the rest of your life," said Jim. "Just don't let it out of your family yet, until you know for sure."

Steve nodded, then looked down at the coffee in his cup. *Don't let it out of your family.* Those words triggered something deep inside him. He'd never known his great-grandfather, or his grandfather, but he knew they had left something dear to them behind in Canada. They left something they had built, worked, loved, and lived. They took a risk by moving to Seattle. Without having anything but family and faith to hold them up, they invested in their future and built what would result in an idyllic childhood for Steve and his siblings.

Steve hadn't expected that conversation with Jim to stir up feelings he didn't realize he had. He had always appreciated his family, especially once he got to college and realized he didn't have the same hardships growing up as many of his peers had. This situation had now become more than a business opportunity. It was more than just a career move. It was more complicated than that. It was about family—his lineage and legacy.

Later that day, Steve called his dad and told him he wanted to come home for the weekend to talk to him more seriously about getting into the business. Don was unusually quiet on the other end of the line. "Hello? Dad? You still there?" asked Steve.

"Yeah, I'm still here," answered Don. Then he continued in a less-than-approving tone. "Well," Don sighed. "Steve, I think you need to talk to Dick Franck or Jack Powell."

Dick and Jack were co-owners of Sound Oil. Despite the fact that Sound Oil was one of Genesee's biggest industry competitors, Don considered Dick and Jack friends and allies against the gas company. Their opinions would be valuable, since they had weathered the same obstacles that Don had, having been in business since 1950. They would be able to give Steve realistic insight about where the industry was headed.

A few days later, Steve sat on the other side of a big wooden desk in Dick's office at Sound Oil. Dick leaned back in his chair, his feet crossed on top of his desk and his fingers linked behind his head. He reminisced about the good ol' days of the '50s, before natural gas, before the oil crisis, and before oil prices had gotten so high. Dick agreed with Don that the industry was diminishing and believed it would never be as good as it once had been. He went on and on painting a dismal picture of the future until Steve finally asked point-blank, "So, are you saying this isn't a viable business for me to get into?"

Dick laughed. He laughed in a way that embarrassed Steve, making him think he had just asked a stupid question. Dick's hands flew out from behind his head. He put his feet on the ground, leaned toward Steve, and when he was done laughing, he said, "Of course it is!" Now Steve could laugh a little, and Dick went on to say, "We might be losing accounts to gas, but so what! It's still a good business. It makes good money."

So what! It was funny to Steve the way Dick had said that. He wondered how long it would have taken him to get to that point, if Steve hadn't asked the question. There had been so many brushes with death in the heating oil business, it was like a cat with nine lives. Yes, the industry was shrinking. Don had made sure Steve understood that. But Genesee was a business that had life in it yet. It was a well-established company with loyal, repeat customers. The company had roots—deep, long, family roots.

"Steve, you really need to think about this," Don urged when he realized the conversation with Dick hadn't gone the way he had expected it would. Don sat back in his chair behind his desk, similar to how Dick sat. "It's just that very few people are putting oil furnaces in anymore. It's a consolidating industry," Don told him again, raising his voice a bit to make sure Steve understood the hardship.

It was obvious to Steve that this was an emotional issue for his dad. "But Dad, it's still a viable business, and a good solid company," Steve argued.

"It's just not like it used to be," replied Don, letting out a sigh. His gaze went to the framed picture of himself and his fellow industry leaders standing with Senator Joel Pritchard after they lobbied in Washington, D.C., that sat on his desk. "You're an established stockbroker. The money business is where the money is. There isn't going to be any money in the oil business for much longer. It won't sustain you."

Steve paused for a moment. Though Don clearly thought Steve hadn't been listening to him about the business, the fact was that Steve *had* been listening. He'd always known there was nothing easy about running a heating oil company. It wasn't a glamorous business, and Steve had never really pictured himself in any part of it. It was only after talking to Jim Coon about the emotional side of things, and then Dick Franck about the business piece, that the idea had taken root as more of an actual possibility than an exploration.

But this was a big deal. Did he really want to do this? Over the past five years he'd been working so hard to build his book of clients with Dain Bosworth. Was he actually considering abandoning the life he'd created in Portland?

The following Friday after work, Steve went with his co-worker Kevin Sahli to the Veritable Quandary in downtown Portland, just around the corner from their office. The

Quandary, with its unique skinny shape, classic old brick walls, and high ceilings, had become one of Steve's favorite places for both beers at the bar and brunch in the garden patio.

Kevin was a few years older than Steve and played a bit of a mentor role for him at Dain Bosworth. He had several more years of experience, and Steve valued his advice. Over beers that night at the Quandary, Steve mentioned his own personal quandary.

Kevin listened, then said, "Steve, why are you working so hard to build your book of business from business owners, when you have access to business ownership right at your feet? Most of the clients you represent are successful business owners because they worked really hard to build their business. It's hard to build a business from nothing. But you have one already built and running."

This was all true. Genesee wasn't a glamorous business, but it was a good business. Maybe having grown up around it, Steve had taken its existence and proximity for granted.

As the bartender put the Widmer Hefeweizen down in front of him, Steve watched a stream of foam spill over and run down the side of the frosty pint glass. If he did decide to move, this was what he would miss most—Portland. It had become known for its brew pubs and live band venues. It had healthy businesses and people with an outdoor adventure mentality. Steve fit right in and felt at home in Portland. By now he had his favorite watering holes in his adopted city: the Brasserie Montmartre, the Bagdad Theater, the Kennedy School. Portland had such great nightlife. He looked up at the neon VQ sign on the brick wall above the mirror behind the bar and got a little nostalgic.

In a way, he wished his dad would have just said, "Steve, it's time for the third generation to step up and run this company." But his dad didn't say that. What Don said was, "Well, I still don't think you ought to do this, but if it's really what you want, I'll support you. Just know this: if it goes under, it's not on me!" Don's words weren't exactly encouragement, but Steve knew what he meant. He knew his dad just didn't want to do anything that would be perceived as shoving his son into the company. He knew that Don wanted his kids to be free to make their own choices. In the most endearing way, Steve's dad just really didn't want his kids to fail. In this industry, Don knew that failing was very possible.

Steve continued to agonize over the decision, which he felt would change the trajectory of his whole life. When all this time he had envisioned getting married and having kids in Portland, working as a stockbroker in a tall building downtown, he now had to imagine an alternative scenario—living in Seattle, doing exactly as his dad had done. How could he choose? How would he know which was the right path to follow?

Multiple times a day this predicament invaded his thoughts. Between clients, driving home from work, or lying awake at night he prayed about what to do. He prayed for direction, for a sign of some sort. "Just don't let it out of your family" were the words of his good friend, Jim Coon. "You owe it to your family to give it a shot," said another friend. Steve had been hearing those words cycling faintly yet relentlessly through his thoughts like the constant drip of a leaky faucet. Finally, Steve attributed that to divine intervention. That was his sign. He could not let Genesee Fuel out of the family. He had to try. It was time for the third generation.

Although leaving Portland was even harder than he'd thought it would be, moving back to Seattle actually turned out to be easier than Steve expected. It felt as if the stars had aligned to welcome him home. He rented a room in a house on the north end of Mercer Island, which was a short commute across the I-90 floating bridge to the office in Rainier Valley. He had been introduced to his roommates through friends also involved with the leadership of Young Life. Although he had just met them upon moving into the house, he knew immediately they would become lifelong friends. The house was a hub of activity. Someone was always stopping by to hang out, and (little did Steve know at the time) his roommates would soon introduce him to his future wife.

Steve moved in June, just as summer arrived, and he quickly realized what he had been missing. Steve had grown up on boats. He was driving a boat before he could drive a car. He'd learned to waterski behind a 1974 Reinell named *Rascal*, and had spent countless hours pulling waterskiers behind the subsequent Sea Rays, *Rascal II* and then *Rascal III*. Now he was in close proximity of the *Rascal IV*, which Don claimed was the last family speedboat he would buy.

Steve's transition at work was a bit more difficult. He knew he had a lot to learn. But luckily for Steve, when he arrived on his first day in his suit and tie—just as he had done at Dain Bosworth, and just as his dad had done every day of his career—he wasn't handed a broom, as Don had been. Instead, he started out with the title of credit manager, since the current one, Gail Hermann, a trusted employee since 1971, was set to retire.

Steve hoped to spend the next few years in training, learning from his dad and eventually moving into the president role. Don, however, didn't have an example of how to transition someone into leadership. Don had simply learned various roles in the business by doing them: driving the truck, handling sales and credit, and so forth. When Gordon died suddenly, Don just had to figure out how to be the one in charge. So Don trained Steve the same way he had been trained. He let him figure it out.

During his first year back in Seattle, while Steve learned his role in the business, he also figured out his romantic life. He had been introduced to Tami Freudenberg soon after he'd moved back. Steve was attracted to Tami right away. She had shoulder-length brown hair, a nice smile, and an easygoing personality. She was a Christian; volunteered for Young Life; played soccer for fitness and fun; was from Bellingham, Washington; and had graduated from Western Washington University. Although Steve was interested in dating Tami, their inter-action had always been a bit awkward, because Tami's room-mate wanted to date Steve, and Steve knew that. So for a year, they all just remained friends.

Then, one Friday evening after work, the group of friends gathered at Steve's house. It was midsummer, and Seattle had been having a stretch of gorgeous warm weather, which ele-vated everyone's mood. The house had a deck with a peek-a-boo view of the lake, and the conversation on their deck that evening turned to waterskiing.

On Lake Washington, the best time for waterskiing is always in the early morning hours. That is when the lake is smooth, and the only boats out there are skiers. Of the people in the room willing to get up early on a Saturday morning to go wa-terskiing, Tami was one of them. The other two were already a couple, so when the four of them made a plan to meet at the boat at five thirty the next morning, Steve hoped this would be something of a first date.

When Saturday morning rolled around, Steve woke up at seven o'clock in a panic. After their house gathering the night before, the guys had ended up going to the Roanoke, the neighborhood bar on Mercer Island. Steve had gotten home late and slept though his alarm, which meant the three friends he had planned on meeting at five thirty were left stranded, at the boat without a boat driver. Steve felt horrible. He thought he'd blown it with Tami. He immediately called her, apologized, and asked if he could make it up to her by buying her lunch. As it turned out, that lunch became their official first date.

Within the first six months of dating, everyone—both Steve and Tami's families and all their friends—saw it was a perfect match. A year and a half later, Steve and Tami were engaged, and in May 1995, they married in Tami's home town of Bellingham.

Sadly, Grandma Katie passed away at age ninety-one, just a few months before Steve and Tami's wedding. Although she was never able to completely shake her bouts of depression, she had come to believe she was blessed beyond measure— and she was. In the final minutes before Katie slipped into a coma, Anita, who might have had the most difficult role as daughter-in-law, stroked Katie's forehead and cheeks, telling her over and over how much she was loved.

By the following spring, three years after Steve had joined Genesee, Don and Steve came up with a plan to officially pass the company baton, making Steve the president and CEO. Don gifted his daughters stock in the company as well, with each of the four kids receiving an equal quarter, though only Steve was given the reins to run it, allowing him the freedom to make decisions without risking family feuds.

Although Don liked to keep a low profile and would have preferred to slide under the radar into retirement, his daughters wanted to celebrate the transition by throwing a big retirement party. They were happy for their dad and proud of Steve. They were also happy, after years of living away, that all the siblings had moved back to the area—Leslie from Alaska,

Karen from San Francisco, and Nanny from Costa Rica. But more than anything, they felt relieved that Steve had stepped up to keep the legacy alive, punctuating the importance of family.

The band hired to play 1950s Big Band music—Don's favorite, from his glory days—quieted when Don took the microphone and stood in front of two hundred of his closest friends at the Washington Athletic Club. He thanked everyone for coming, then made a joke. "You know, there's a saying about family businesses. It goes: 'The first generation creates it, the second generation maintains it, and the third generation runs it into the ground.'" Don loved making an audience laugh. For Steve, the old saying was funny in a way that required an obligatory laugh, but at this point, he was all in, and determined to disprove that statement.

Just as soon as the STEVE CLARK, PRESIDENT plaque was erected on his office door, Steve started to earn his executive MBA at the University of Washington. Getting an MBA was something he'd always wanted to do but never felt he could. He had started working right away after his undergraduate degree and stopping to become a full-time student again hadn't seemed feasible. Now he was a newlywed who had a company to run and a mortgage to pay, which didn't seem ideal either, but as Steve had learned over the past several years, the timing is never perfect. If something is a priority, you just have to dive in and make it work. His dad, of course, gave him all kinds of encouragement to continue his studies.

The more Steve studied, observed, and learned about business, the more excited he got about the future. For one of his projects at school, he researched a heating oil product that was more environmentally friendly than standard diesel. If he was going to take the company into the future, he felt that he needed to look ahead to see what heating options were coming down the pike.

In the mid-1990s, biodiesel was still in the experimental phase. But it was lower in carbon emissions than standard heating oil, making it better for the environment. If it could someday be used as an alternative to standard petroleum heating oil, Steve wanted to be in on it from the start. He knew that forward thinking and changing along with cultural perspectives was the only way to keep the company relevant. Steve wrote up his project with specifics for implementing biodiesel within the company in the near future.

Once he'd graduated from the University of Washington with his executive MBA, Steve was ready to make his mark. One thing he'd come to understand during his first few years with Genesee and as a result of his studies was that his dad was right. The business as it currently stood didn't have a very long future ahead, not with heating oil alone.

CHAPTER NINETEEN

1999–2013

The only rock I know that stays steady,
the only institution I know that works, is the family.
—LEE IACOCCA

IN JUNE 1999, STEVE TURNED HIS ATTENTION AWAY FROM THE business and toward family matters. That month, he and Tami would welcome their first child. This wouldn't be the first grandchild for Don and Anita born in the family—Leslie and her husband, Trip, had two girls, Katie and Caroline, and Karen had one daughter, Samantha.

Steve always wanted both a boy and girl eventually, so prior to the birth, he and Tami had chosen not to know the gender of their first baby. Throughout the whole labor and delivery, gender didn't even enter Steve's mind. All he thought about—prayed for—was a healthy baby and a safe delivery. When that happened, and it was a boy, Steve was overwhelmed with emotions he didn't see coming.

He looked at his son with such pride, not only for himself, but also for the men in his family lineage. He and Tami had picked the name long before the birth. If they had a boy, he would be Eli Silas Clark, named after his great-great-grandfather, the entrepreneur, Canadian farmer, immigrant, and source of original funding for the now-third-generation family business.

When Don walked into the hospital room and was introduced to his grandson for the first time, Steve watched his dad's eyes get watery. He knew it meant a lot to him that they gave the baby a family name. As an only child, Don had been a single link in the chain of Clark boys. He wondered if Don was tearing up because he was overwhelmed with joy at seeing his grandson or if he was thinking about his own father and his grandfather whose name this baby how held. Either way, they all must have been smiling in heaven at that moment.

Back at work, Steve sat at his big oak desk in the office that had once been his dad's and his grandfather's before that. He looked around and noted what had remained the same throughout the six decades of business in that office. The building, when you first walked in, still had that faint gas station smell, but it had grown less pungent over the years since heating oil smells less vapory and more oily than gasoline. The phones still rang nonstop on cold days, and the trucks still rolled out with full tanks every morning around seven thirty. The industry was still dependent on weather, the cost of oil for fuel still fluctuated, and they still worked hard to keep every customer.

He looked at the framed picture of his baby boy, Eli, who was already growing so fast, and thought about change.

"Change is the law of life. And those who look only to the past or present are certain to miss the future," said John F. Kennedy. A true statement, when Steve thought about it. Despite the physical smells, sounds, and routines that had remained the same, embracing change and looking to the future were the only reasons he was sitting there today. It was Si's willingness to change his nationality and to go from small-town rural living to city life. It was Gordon and Russ's courage to change products for the future of their business; it was Don's foresight to change the narrative from "We're done" to "We'll grow through acquisitions."

In the fall of 1999, the term "Y2K" had instilled fear in many people over what would happen on New Year's Eve, when the dates on the computers—which society had come to depend on—turned over into the twenty-first century, the start of a new century. Steve knew he could not be fearful of the future. He had to take what had worked in the past—the basic principles on which his company was built, as laid out by his grandfather, view the present with a fresh perspective, and look to the future. He had the challenging task of bringing Genesee into the twenty-first century. For Steve, this meant the pressure was on.

Turning his attention toward the business and its future, Steve started with a mathematical approach. How many customers were switching to natural gas, and what was the annual rate of loss? He calculated: *Even if that number doubles, the busi-*

ness will be fine for another fifteen years, and that's without buying other companies to expand our reach. By his calculations, the rate of loss wasn't rapid enough to worry about in the short term.

It was freeing to know where things stood. Now Steve knew he had a large window of opportunity—and ideas to boot. He would continue to acquire other companies and think about adding products in addition to oil, but first he wanted to focus on the brand standard.

Genesee trucks had carried the company's brand all over Seattle for over half a century. Customers often said that when they saw the big red truck with white lettering outlined in black, they had positive feelings, associating the trucks and their design with the arrival of warmth to their homes. But on close inspection of the trucks, Steve noticed that each wore a slightly different shade of red and slightly different lettering. Harmonizing the company's logo became one of Steve's first efforts in brand management. As it turned out, it would be one of the easiest.

Standardizing the brand when it came to procedures and protocols would prove to be more difficult. Every employee had their own way of doing things, which meant there was too much variation in the way transactions were handled and in the treatment that customers received. Steve saw a lack of efficiency, and he also wanted more consistency in the way employees greeted customers, documented jobs, answered the phones, and so on. If seven people were making omelets and didn't have a list of ingredients or specifics on how to make that omelet, each would turn out very different.

Many Genesee employees had gotten used to doing things on their own terms under Don's regime and had gotten stuck in the mindset of "because we've always done it that way." In some cases, that worked. But Steve wanted to raise standards across the whole company. He wanted to make sure the Genesee name was synonymous with high-quality customer service, a principle it was founded on.

That required changes that many employees didn't want to make. It was an awkward situation since some of Genesee's employees had been working there since Steve was a little boy, and now he was their boss. But Steve had to focus on long-term goals. He could not step in and run the company exactly as his dad had. He was his own person and a different kind of leader. As a businessman, he more closely resembled his grandfather Gordon—a deep thinker and a detail-oriented person.

Steve knew these changes would be hard, but he also knew they needed to happen. Pulling concepts he'd learned in graduate school and applying them to the business, he gently and intentionally made the changes he saw fit and established his authority as a thoughtful leader at the same time.

In the early 2000s, Steve expanded Genesee's services to include more HVAC (heating, ventilating, and air conditioning); the company had done a bit of installation work such as replacing oil furnaces or adding air conditioning in the past, but only when customers asked for it. Steve wanted to bump up this part of the business. He wanted Genesee to be the company that came to mind when people thought about all things regarding home heating and cooling comfort.

In doing that, he created an installations department as a division of Genesee Fuel & Heating. But instead of just focusing on oil furnace installations, he decided he would also install gas furnaces for customers wanting to switch from oil to natural gas. This was a big change. For so long the oil industry thought of natural gas as being the enemy, and they'd wanted nothing to do with the changeovers.

Steve took a different perspective—one that was not highly popular with anyone in the oil industry but particularly his employees. They didn't want to sell gas furnaces or to service them. They wanted to remain loyal to oil, as they always had been. Under Don's tenure, when a customer switched to natural gas, Don took it as an insult and walked away, frustrated and irritated. The employees who'd been in the industry for as long as Steve had been alive held on to that attitude.

But their mission didn't change. Genesee was still a heating oil company, and its main business was in supplying that product to its customers. They would always encourage oil, but in Steve's progressive thinking, if the company was going to lose a customer to natural gas, they might as well get one final sale—by installing their gas furnace and potentially keeping them as an HVAC maintenance customer.

Although this was yet another hurdle Steve had to get over, he forged ahead. While he did that, he also focused on creating a more positive culture among the employees within the walls of the company. He bought lunch for everyone at staff meetings, celebrated birthdays with the employee's cake of choice, and added a holiday gift exchange, to name a few.

As the HVAC department grew, so did the faith Steve's employees placed in him as a leader.

Acquiring other heating oil companies had been Don's strategy, and Steve agreed that this was still an important way that Genesee would broaden its reach. Ironically, in the early 2000s, the next acquisition opportunity put Don and Steve at opposite corners. Bowman Oil was a company that Don and others in the industry hated to compete against. The owner, Bob Bowman, tended to ruffle feathers among industry leaders by slashing prices and running big flashy ads.

When Steve told his dad of his plans to buy the company, Don's response was, "You're making a mistake." Historically, Don had always done business only with people who shared his business style and had handled customers similarly. These transactions were personal to him, whereas Steve was open to taking a different perspective. Steve thought that if he bought Bowman, he could actually learn something from them.

Don didn't hesitate to give his opinion, and Steve, on hearing it, didn't argue. He didn't get mad or tell him to stay out of it. He heard his dad out, then simply didn't take his advice. Steve was going to do things his own way. So, with caution, he went ahead with the acquisition, and in the end, they did learn something from Bowman in terms of marketing and being more price competitive. These things were exactly what they hadn't liked about competing against them, but they were good strategies. That acquisition forced Genesee to become nimbler and more aggressive, and in time, those would be concepts Steve would apply to other aspects of the business.

By 2008, the economy was as good as it had ever been, if not better. The price of oil was low, and Steve was again in negotiations, this time to buy Laurelhurst Oil. Laurelhurst was attractive to Steve because it had developed a reputation among environmentally conscious customers for its biodiesel. Genesee had just begun providing biodiesel to its customers as an option as well, calling it Bioheat—as it was a blend of standard heating oil and biodiesel—but they hadn't yet marketed it, as Laurelhurst had.

While buying any company was always a risk, just weeks before closing the deal with Laurelhurst, the risk increased dramatically when the price of oil shot up from less than $40 per barrel to $150 per barrel. Not only was Genesee about to take on a million-dollar debt, but now Steve would have 30 percent more customers that he hoped would continue to heat with oil versus switch to natural gas.

Don, who tended to take the conservative approach, said, "The price is too high. You'll never make money on that deal." Steve knew there was risk, but Laurelhurst had plenty of offers from other local companies. The only reason they wanted to sell to Genesee was because Genesee was the only company that was already selling biodiesel and committed to continuing to do so. If Genesee didn't follow through with this deal, another company would snatch them up.

Part of Steve's thinking was that biodiesel was the future of heating oil. Efforts to combat global warming had gone on for years, but more recently, there'd been talk surrounding heating oil and its carbon emissions. Steve believed in environmental sustainability as a worthy pursuit; in lowering pollutants, cleaner air, and maintaining the beauty of the Northwest. He wanted that for himself, for his kids, and for future generations. But he also wanted sustainability of the business that was not only his legacy but also his livelihood.

Historically, heating oil had been high in carbon output, but Genesee's standard heating oil was now ULSHO (ultra-low sulfur heating oil), which was significantly lower in carbon emissions than the heating oil that been the industry standard in 1970. But still, burning heating oil released carbon that was harmful to the environment. Biodiesel, however, when blended with ULSHO at a ratio of just 20 percent, reduced the carbon output of heating a home to less than that of heating with natural gas. At a 99 percent blend, pollutants are decreased by as much as 80 percent compared to standard heating oil alone. The phrase "Reduce your carbon footprint" would be directly applicable for customers choosing biodiesel. This, Steve thought, was the direction heating oil needed to go if it were going to still be around thirty years from now.

But still, Steve struggled with the decision to move ahead with this purchase. He knew it would be the biggest risk he'd taken. Taking this chance could either lead the company into bankruptcy or it could put them in a position to be on the cutting edge as one of the biggest local fuel companies in Seattle. Despite his dad's discouragement, Steve decided to go ahead and buy Laurelhurst.

Just two weeks later, in late September 2008, Steve was still sweating the purchase, wondering if his dad had been right. The stock market had taken a massive dive—the biggest one since 1929, the year that Gordon and Russ bought the company. The circumstances were eerily similar. Like his grandfather, Steve had no idea at first of how this economic downturn would affect the company, and also like Gordon, he was in debt and feared the worst.

Then, soon after the market crashed, the price of oil also fell. The sudden recession that had caused companies to cut back also caused the demand for oil to decrease drastically. When the demand goes down, so does the price. Over the course of a few months, the price of oil had increased from $40 to $150 per barrel, and then it fell back down to $32. That major price cut allowed Steve some room to breathe. In that difficult economic time, Genesee wouldn't have to raise the price of heating oil for its customers—at least not yet. But winter was just around the corner. Although forecasters were predicting a La Niña (colder than average) year, Steve still held his breath.

Most years, Seattle saw only a trace of snow, where temperatures straddled the freezing point once or twice briefly and precipitation teetered between wet snow and rain. More often than not, the slushy northwest snow arrived for just long enough to cause transportation headaches and disappeared quickly while disappointed kids clutched their unused sleds. Those in the heating business always hope for a cold winter, but this year, given his recent debt, Steve hoped harder than ever that the forecasters' predictions of colder weather would come true.

It had been a typical fall, but starting in mid-December 2008, just a few days before most schools let out for the holiday break, La Niña arrived. The temperatures dropped, and the snow hit. It wasn't the typical Seattle snow, which fell heavy and fast, glued together in clumps, their hexagon shapes mutilated by the water that bound them. This snow fell consistently in tiny, delicate, six-sided snowflakes, just like the kind children cut out and hang in their classroom windows—and it kept falling. The snowflakes fell gently and relentlessly, beginning an extended, record-setting, cold and snowy winter.

While schools closed early for the winter break, Genesee's drivers chained up their truck tires and ramped up their deliveries. Although Don was typically annoyed by inconvenience of getting around in the snow, this time he leaned back in his chair at his desk (now relocated to the basement of Genesee) and chuckled. "Well, I still think you paid too much for Laurelhurst," he said, "but it looks like you'll get lucky with the weather this year."

Steve let out his breath and agreed. Seattle hadn't seen a winter like this in at least a decade. Whether it was luck or an answer to his pleading prayers, Steve was grateful.

By 2010, family gatherings at the Clark family house on Mercer Island had become chaotic. Steve and Tami had another boy, Josiah Steven, and a girl, Anna Kathleen, to complete their family. The number of total grandkids for Don and Anita had grown to twelve. While this commotion brought mostly joy, there were heartaches, too. Karen's second baby girl, Erin Elizabeth, lived for only six days. It was a heartbreaking whirlwind that devastated the whole family. But through the ordeal, the family pulled closer together, just as they had a few years earlier when they learned Anita had colon cancer. Then, they'd rallied around a meal rotation and nursed her through until she came out the other side, cancer free.

While family life was moving and changing fast, so was the fuel industry. Steve found himself needing to keep up the pace. Taking a break from buying companies, Steve started thinking beyond the city of Seattle and even beyond the collar of suburbs that surrounded it. Where the gas lines ended, propane was becoming the popular choice for home heating in newly constructed neighborhoods. Like heating oil, propane was delivered via trucks to residents with propane-powered furnaces and appliances. With the systems already in place, Steve just needed to find a supplier and buy a propane truck.

So, that's what he did. In 2011, Genesee Propane, a division of Genesee Fuel & Heating, was born. Around the same time, Steve decided the company needed another update to its name. As with clothing and hairstyles, vocabulary goes in and out of fashion. Replacing the word *fuel* with *energy* was something he'd thought about for a while, and now with the company's expanded service department, the addition of propane, and the increased distribution of Bioheat, it felt like the right time.

"Genesee Energy" would be a name that not only reflected the current business, including propane, HVAC, and Bioheat, but also maintained its identity as it had been recognized for nearly ninety years in the neighborhood as a heating oil distributer.

In the fall of 2013, the whole family flew to Hawaii to celebrate Don and Anita's fifty-fifth wedding anniversary over Thanksgiving. It was a special time. Anita's cancer had come back, but she had just completed chemotherapy, and her prognosis was good.

Somewhere along the way Don, the patriarch, had started a tradition that involved a peppermint pig—a tradition adapted from one that began in Saratoga Springs, New York, in the late 1800s. Many cultures see the pig as a symbol of prosperity and good health. With this in mind, the Saratoga Springs candymakers created a small, bright-pink peppermint candy in the shape of a pig. Although the ritual was customarily practiced after a Christmas dinner, the Clark family did it every year at Thanksgiving. According to the tradition, the candy pig was placed in a small black velvet bag and passed around the table. While holding the pig, each person struck a blow at the pig through the bag with a small silver-plated hammer while reflecting on what they were most thankful for that year.

That Thanksgiving in Hawaii as they passed around the pig, those surrounding the table felt a great sense of pride. This family had come a long way in a hundred years, all the way from their old Canadian farming roots. Steve looked at his kids, his nieces and nephews. Would the company still be around when they were of age? That was always Steve's goal: to keep the company going for at least his career. Many aspects of the business were the same as they'd been when his grandfather ran it, yet much was different. He'd had to change, add, subtract, and jump curves just to stay alive. But the company had survived, and it was perhaps more stable now than it had ever been.

At this point, the question was less about whether the company would be around for the next generation and more about whether the members of that generation would choose it—if it would still be a viable company by then. Looking at those kids, as young as they were, Steve couldn't picture any of them involved in running the company. But then again, he hadn't thought he would ever get involved, and here he was. He'd been running and growing Genesee for twenty-three years, and it still had plenty of life.

CHAPTER TWENTY

2013–2021

Never, never, never give up.
—WINSTON CHURCHILL

IT WOULD BE NICE IF MAKING PROGRESS WERE LINEAR, BUT it's not. Off and on over the years, as far back as the 1970s, the City of Seattle has put pressure on the heating oil industry in various ways that have caused stress and worry for all within it. Recently, the City of Seattle approved a plan to reach citywide carbon neutrality by 2050. If fully implemented, the city's plan to replace all fossil fuels (natural gas, heating oil, and coal) with hydroelectric power—which in Washington State is plentiful—would eventually drive companies like Genesee Energy out of business. Its first action item directly targeted residential heating oil because the city government—along with many people—held the common perception that heating oil is dirty.

For years, Steve had been offering biodiesel blends to customers as a way to lower carbon output in the interest of improving our air quality and decreasing greenhouse gases. But biodiesel was more expensive than standard petroleum heating oil, so customers had to opt in. Therefore, many did not. A good chunk of Genesee Energy customers were income restricted, either older people in homes they had lived in for decades—retired, living on social security—or young families in old homes with plenty of other expenses. Another reason, according to a survey, that many of Genesee's current customers were not choosing Bioheat was because they didn't have enough information about it to make the switch.

In spring of 2013, Steve's youngest sister, Andrea—that is, I, the author—approached Steve asking for a job.

"I'll do anything," I begged. "Well, almost anything," I added, remembering Dad's broom story. "I just want a job. And not a volunteer job, a real job." I had been a teacher before having my three kids, but I had been home with them since 2000, volunteering in the school, at church, and most recently, substitute teaching.

"OK, I can give you a job. We have plenty of data entry to do," Steve replied. He hesitated before he continued, "But what if I have to fire you?"

I laughed, but when Steve didn't laugh with me, I realized he was asking me a serious question. "Well, I've never been fired before, so I'm hoping it won't come to that," I said. Then I understood he wasn't questioning my work ethic. He just wanted to make sure I got it that he was still the CEO and that I wasn't going to move in and start bossing people around. Since I had no intention of doing that, I continued to explain myself. "Really, this is just to help me get into the working world so I can figure out what I really want to do. I have no professional experience other than teaching, and I'm not sure I want to go back to that."

Steve nodded and replied, "So it's to help you build your resume."

"Yes," I said, relieved he understood. That was exactly how I saw it, even if I wasn't able to put it into words. I was in my early forties and searching for direction. I felt there was a part of me—a purpose deep within—that had been left untapped. My days had been feeling monotonous, and I yearned for something deeper. It's not that I felt finished raising kids— they were still young. And I never for one minute regretted staying home with my kids; it was exactly where I wanted to be at the time. In fact, I think I'd pursued a career in teaching because it seemed like a good training for motherhood. But when my youngest started kindergarten, I felt a sense of loss and longing for my purpose. With potentially decades of professional life ahead of me, I didn't just want to get back to work. I wanted to find my calling.

What started as data entry quickly evolved into updating the company website, creating a social media presence, and then adding content in an effort to educate people about the benefits of Bioheat.

"This is such an amazing product. I don't understand why everyone isn't using it," I told Steve one day.

"It's been an uphill battle. It's hard convincing people that anything related to heating oil is good. It's been years of the same message that heating oil is dirty. People are skeptical and slow to change."

But I decided I had to try something. I was an educator, after all, and here was an area where people needed educating. After a bit of investigation, I figured out that most people change out their furnace either when the furnace quits on them (which, in the case of heating oil furnaces, can be upward of fifty years) or when new homeowners buy a house that has oil heat. In that case, when a real estate agent lists that home, the heating oil furnace is often a negative selling point. When potential buyers look at a home with oil heat, their buying agent likely tells them it is no problem, they can always change it out to natural gas or an electric heat pump. What they don't often say is how much that costs—about fifteen thousand dollars.

By educating the agents, I would attempt to change their strategy. I created a twenty-minute PowerPoint presentation and set up appointments at local real estate agents' office meetings. Before getting into the meat of the presentation, I always tried to make the audience laugh—a trick I learned in my teaching days, both to calm my own nerves and to gain my students' attention. "I used to teach elementary school children," I began, "but this should be easier because I'm pretty sure you're not going to be throwing pencils or shooting rubber bands at each other."

I went on to suggest that in their listings, instead of an oil tank and furnace being a negative selling point, they could be turned into a positive. "Biodiesel is a renewable fuel in the same category as wind and solar," I explained, while projecting a slide showing the fossil fuels of natural gas, petroleum heating oil, and coal on one side of the solid line, and the renewable energy sources of wind, solar, geothermal, hydropower, and biomass (which includes biodiesel) on the other side. I continued to explain that by putting even the lowest blend of Bioheat into the tank, the seller could market the house as emitting less carbon into the environment than its next-door neighbor using natural gas. By putting in the highest blend offered, they could market the house as an eco-friendly, green-fuel-heated house.

The presentations were always well received and the feedback positive, but unfortunately, I found that making change in this area was like moving a pile of gravel with chopsticks. Most of the agents agreed that the argument was thought provoking, but others looked at me like I was telling them that smoking cigarettes was actually good for their health. This was such a different story than the one they had always believed—that heating oil in any form was dirty.

Meanwhile, the City of Seattle continued to press. Several carbon tax proposals in recent years had failed, but barely. Steve knew the city was not giving up, and it also wasn't recognizing biodiesel as a low-carbon or potentially carbon-free option in its purest form. Although Steve knew he would not go down without a fight, he was also thinking he needed to prepare himself for a major shift in his business. He recognized that in ten years, if his company was to make it that far, it would have to look very different. He knew he couldn't sacrifice the present for the future because heating oil was his bread and butter—the HVAC and propane divisions of Genesee weren't making any money yet. But he also couldn't sacrifice the future for the present. The trend in energy was shifting. Steve knew that somehow, he had to shift with it.

What company can stay afloat for over a century without a few major shifts? The Kodak company dominated the photographic industry for most of the twentieth century. In 1975, they were on the cutting edge and actually developed the first digital camera. But for fear of hurting the company's most profitable product—photographic film—it withheld marketing the digital camera. By the time Kodak figured out the trend was not reversing, it was too late, and in 2012 the company filed for bankruptcy.

In 2018, while Steve was still figuring but hadn't yet come up with a solid solution, he heard about another buying opportunity in Bremerton, Washington, on the Kitsap Peninsula, just across the Puget Sound from Seattle. Cooper Fuel was for sale. Steve hadn't been looking to buy another heating oil company; in fact, he was thinking he should steer away from the fuel that seemed to have a looming expiration date. But Dave Cooper was looking to retire from the business he'd inherited from his father, Clyde Cooper, who started the company in 1953. As in the past, most of these acquisitions came down to relationships, and this one was no different. Don Clark knew Clyde Cooper through his industry acquaintances. Although Clyde was now gone, his son was running the company. Because of this connection and the kinship they shared in both being family businesses, Dave Cooper declined another offer of sale and agreed to do business with Steve.

The ferry pulled away from Colman Dock and sounded its

loud, low departure horn. Inside the upper deck, Steve watched as the Seattle skyline slowly came into full view, then started to fade into the horizon as the ferry moved toward Bremerton. Not a bad commute, Steve thought.

Approaching Bremerton on the ferry brought back a flood of memories for Steve, who had ridden this route many times as a boy. The grandparents on his mother Anita's side lived in Silverdale, Kitsap County, across the street from the beach of Dyes Inlet. Steve, his siblings, and all his cousins referred to this set of grandparents as Grandma and Grandpa Camper, simply because they had a camper parked on the lawn in their back yard. The ferry ride, hitting golf balls from their front yard into the bay and then scouring the beach to find them at low tide, playing in and around that camper, and climbing on top of the refrigerator to get into the attic—it had always been a treat to visit his grandparents there.

Cooper Fuel hadn't previously offered Bioheat, so buying this company increased Genesee Energy's customer base in standard heating oil only. But this was still a step in the right direction. Broadening the geographic footprint of the company to outside the city boundary not only minimized potential damage to the business posed by the City of Seattle, it also gave Genesee greater exposure for the future of Bioheat and propane as well.

By the summer of 2019, Steve felt really good about the Cooper acquisition, but sure enough, more bad news soon came regarding heating oil in Seattle. In August 2019, Mayor Jenny Durkan proposed a heating oil tax of twenty-four cents per gallon as well as a requirement that by 2028, all heating oil equipment be replaced by electric heat pumps. Biodiesel was not mentioned and would therefore also be taxed. Steve religiously followed the local news and had known this was coming down the pike, but when the specifics were released, he felt paralyzed.

Steve clasped his hands together, put them on top of his head, leaned back in his chair and looked up at the ceiling. For the first time ever, there was a date in black and white that could very well be the end of Genesee Energy in Seattle. The year 2028 was less than a decade away, and it was also the year Genesee Energy would turn ninety-nine years old. This was too soon, and that was all Steve could think about. He had diversified the company by adding propane, expanding his geographical footprint beyond the city of Seattle, and offering renewable, biodegradable Bioheat. He was doing all he could think of to do, but still, this news was a blow.

A week later, he found himself at a city council meeting, waiting patiently for his turn to make a comment when the opportunity was given to the general public. He was nervous. He knew he had one shot, and his window of opportunity would be less than thirty seconds long. He had to make his point clear. He also felt alone. The other local heating oil companies were in support of fighting the tax but didn't understand at the time how biodiesel could help. Steve was not only going to bat for his livelihood, but for his industry and his customers, too. He had one argument.

When the time came, Steve was called on to speak.

"I understand that the tax has provisions to help people in the lowest income bracket to pay for the conversion of their oil furnaces, but what about the next bracket of people?" Steve began. "According to your data, that leaves five percent of homeowners in Seattle who will be forced to come up with fifteen thousand dollars each to change out their systems. That adds up to $250 million collectively. If those people can't afford to pay for new systems by your deadline of 2028, who is going to foot the bill?"

Silence followed. But a moment later, one of the council members said, "Where is this guy getting that number? Can someone check into that?"

A member of the Office of Sustainability and Environment replied, "Those are our numbers."

Steve continued. "I'm proposing you accept biodiesel as a transition fuel, exempting it from the tax. Tanks can be filled with biodiesel and used on the existing heating oil equipment without costly change-outs. This would allow us to move in the same direction of lowering carbon output while also giving people more time to come up with the money they will need to change out their heating equipment when they are ready."

In November 2019, Mayor Durkan signed into law the carbon tax that would take effect in 2020. Excluded from the tax was biodiesel. Steve had made his point, clearly. The city council had heard him. He knew there would still be hurdles to overcome, but for now he could breathe a bit easier. This victory gave him time to plan and space to move forward with what the next decade would look like for Genesee Energy. Eventually, electric heat pumps would likely take over all heating oil equipment in Seattle—and probably transcend its borders. Steve knew this and had come to accept it. But he also knew that there was opportunity in this difficulty, and perhaps most importantly, he understood that change is the only way that a family business will survive and thrive through a century and beyond.

A few months later, Steve walked out the back door of the building on Genesee Street and paused. He had been on his way to the "West Wing," fifteen feet away, where his office was located now. The annex had once been a detached garage, but with every acquisition, Genesee gained employees. The company's headquarters had finally run out of working spaces. Repurposing the garage, the West Wing was now both Steve's office and the conference room, where Christmas parties, spring barbeques, and office staff meetings were held.

As Steve stood halfway between the original office building and his new space, he looked at the loading rack his grandfather Gordon had engineered, still straddling the tanks buried deep below. Each generation that stood on that property had contributed something valuable and different. Si gave his money and encouragement, Gordon and Russ jumped in with a vision and hard work, Don cultivated perseverance and added character, and now Steve brought his courage and forward thinking. Each, guided by faith, walked into unknown circumstances and overcame. Each took a close look inward to find their true selves, and with tenacity, dared greatly to pursue. Each found the business as a means but held family as paramount.

Each generation also made their own changes, but despite them all, every morning the trucks still lined up at the loading rack to fill their tanks before their daily deliveries. Steve walked by that rack multiple times a day, but every once in a while, he stopped in awe and wonder. He envisioned his grandfather standing there in his narrow metal-rimmed glasses, his ears sticking out a bit from his round head, a tiny pink rose tucked into the lapel of his three-piece, pin-striped suit. Standing there, Gordon would have nodded and cracked a gentle smile at Steve, affirming his pride.

EPILOGUE

ON THAT OCTOBER DAY IN 2013 WHEN I WALKED THROUGH the back door of the Genesee Fuel & Heating Company, it smelled and looked the same as I remembered, though I hadn't been there in years. Immediately I envisioned my grandfather Gordon, my dad Don, and my brother Steve, walking through the same door for the same reason I had—to report for my first day of work.

Like my sisters Leslie and Karen, I hadn't worked at Genesee as a teenager, the way our brother had. But occasionally our dad would employ us at home to help with seasonal mailers. We would sit in front of the TV, likely watching *Little House on the Prairie*, folding letters, stuffing envelopes, and putting on address labels while earning five cents per envelope.

Whether we worked at the building on Genesee Street or not, we all grew up understanding that cold winters were good, that customers switching to natural gas was bad, and that if we talked on the phone too long with our friends during the winter months, we might get in trouble.

"Get off the phone—you're tying up the line!" Dad's booming voice would echo down the hall, causing us to hang up the phone without time for much explanation. Minutes later, on a call, we'd hear him ask a customer, "Did you push the reset button?" as he helped them sort out what their furnace problems might be.

In keeping with the generations that preceded them, a few of the kids in the fourth generation have dipped their toes into the family business in various capacities. Steve's firstborn, Eli, and his second son, Josiah, spent high-school summers doing odd jobs and data entry at the office.

In 2014, my middle son, Henry, chose his great-grandfather Gordon Clark as the subject of his seventh-grade Legacy project. During his research he asked questions like "Why did he leave Canada?" and "What was it like in Seattle back then?" In helping him, I realized what a hardship it must have been for Si and his sons to sell the farm, leave their country of birth, start a business, and survive dire straits all within one difficult year: 1929.

It occurred to me then that my life wouldn't be the same had they not made those choices. We're all influenced not only by our childhood upbringings, but also by the choices our grandparents and great-grandparents made long before our time. We are who we are in part because of them. My grandparents' journeys, successes, failures, faith, and love have influenced my life, the lives of my siblings, and the lives of our children.

Although thoughts of this book began to coalesce the minute I walked through the door in 2013 for my first day of work, I let the idea percolate a bit. In 2015, we said goodbye to my dear mom, Anita Jean Clark, who had fought cancer off and on for over twenty years. Having been with my dad since they were sixteen years old, she held a unique perspective on the family business that I wish I had been able to tap into while writing this book. But her passing brought the realization that if the stories of our parents, grandparents, great-grandparents, and so on aren't written down, a piece of our history dies with them.

In 2016, I started jotting down the stories I'd heard over and over through the years. Those were easy. But I also had pieces of stories, stories with holes, and painful stories, such as the events surrounding my grandfather's death. I liked the idea of putting them all together, but the execution of a cohesive book felt like an insurmountable task. Still, I couldn't let it go. This family business, with its volatile past, meant more to me than I had realized. My dad, now in his eighties and with a sharp memory, became my constant source of encouragement, and my mom, from her classroom in heaven, my angelic motivation.

In 2017, my oldest son, James, focused his school DECA (Distributive Education Clubs of America) marketing project on Genesee's Bioheat. The framework for this project was to choose a company that would be willing to provide information and the access necessary to conduct research, as well as the space to create and execute a proposed marketing plan of action. Not so surprisingly, Genesee wasn't his first choice. James looked for a company with a product that aligned with his interests—which didn't include heating oil and propane. But just as his grandpa, his uncle, and his mom had at first overlooked Genesee's charms, James came to realize this was his family business, too. At his presentation, James proudly explained the backstory of the company his great-grandfather had built and took his DECA report to the state competition.

At the heart of it, this book is a story of an American company and of a family that came to the United States, built, planted roots, and sustained. Although this is our story, it is not unlike the stories of many other families and their businesses. Nordstrom, John L. Scott Real Estate, and Borracchini's Bakery on Rainier Avenue all started in a Seattle of immigrants and are all still running as family businesses with third-generation leadership and ownership.

Not too far out on the horizon, in 2029, is Genesee's one hundredth birthday. Steve has set goals for where he wants the company to be by then and is working toward them. One of his goals is to have all of Genesee's heating oil customers receiving B100 (one hundred percent biodiesel) by then. Like his dad and grandfather, he wants the company to thrive so that if any of the kids want to get involved, they can. Whether this fourth generation travels or stays put, they will know they have a rich family history of entrepreneurial spirit, adventure, perseverance, and faith to not only ground them but to provide an example of weathering storms and finding their way through the hard times in life, which are—as this story shows— inevitable.

ACKNOWLEDGMENTS

Since writing this book required a century of research, I am grateful for the places that collect, organize, and preserve history. These include the Rainier Valley Historical Society, the University of Washington Suzzallo and Allen Libraries, the Museum of History and Industry, HistoryLink.org, and the Provincial Archives of Alberta, all of which provided invaluable context and cultural perspective in writing this book.

A shout out to my Canadian friend Lisa, who spent several days with me in Leduc, Alberta, reading through archives, driving through farmlands, sneaking around abandoned barns, and searching the cemetery until we found my great grandmother's resting place.

In 2016 I took a writing class taught by Nick O'Connell at the Writer's Workshop in Seattle. Nick was the first person who told me I had a strong story with a distinct angle and could one day be published. I can still smell the wine and cheese on the windowsill in that class at the Wallingford Center where my writing career began, with nothing but a big idea and a little encouragement to fuel it.

After completing that class, I had pieces of the story but lacked a concrete structure to tie them all together. Through divine intervention and LinkedIn, I found Sandra Byrd, who coached me on story structure and provided necessary weekly deadlines, helping me bring my first draft manuscript to completion.

The next step—finding a publisher—was a daunting, humbling, and frustrating process, until I found Brooke Warner of She Writes Press. Brooke accepted my first draft manuscript on the condition I go through developmental editing, which led me to Katherine Sharpe, who through multiple rounds of edits helped bring clarity and cohesiveness to my final draft.

Of course, none of the words in this book would have made it onto the page without my dad, his memory, and his stories. Dad drove me around Seattle showing me the apartment where my grandparents met, the house in which he was raised, the corner he'd wait on for his dad, the steps where he met his local hero, and the site of his dad's accident, just to name a few. He read every version I wrote and has exercised more patience with me in this process than I knew he was capable of.

Since my mom is no longer on this earth, my mother-in-law, Carlene, stepped in and offered the motherly love and support I needed. She also read an earlier version and, in character, gave me more positive feedback than I knew what to do with.

I also leaned heavily on my siblings, Leslie, Steve, and Karen, for their memory and perspective. I am grateful that Leslie is the keeper of memorabilia, that Steve was always willing to adjust his schedule whenever I needed time to pick his brain, and that Karen always answers her phone when I need a sister chat.

Finally, I am so thankful for my Watson family. All three of my boys, James, Henry, and Will, have given me so much inspiration and grace while I worked on this book. The pride is cyclical, bouncing from me to them and back to me again. And a huge thank you to Jim, my husband, my life partner, and my biggest fan. I am blessed beyond measure and could not have brought this book to publication without his support.

ABOUT THE AUTHOR

ANDREA WATSON currently lives in her hometown, Mercer Island, Washington, with her husband and three boys. Her favorite thing to do is plan trips and travel as she is always on the hunt for that undiscovered gem of a small town. She also enjoys hiking, skiing, and walking her dog. With her family she loves spending time at their cabin on Lake Chelan, Washington. She began her career as a teacher in special education and English for non-native speakers. After her first child was born, she stayed home to raise her three boys. Soon after her third child entered school, she started working for the family business in the areas of marketing and content writing. It was sitting in that office—the same office her grandfather once sat in—that prompted her to write this book.